SAGE was founded in 1965 by Sara Miller McCune to support the dissemination of usable knowledge by publishing innovative and high-quality research and teaching content. Today, we publish over 900 journals, including those of more than 400 learned societies, more than 800 new books per year, and a growing range of library products including archives, data, case studies, reports, and video. SAGE remains majority-owned by our founder, and after Sara's lifetime will become owned by a charitable trust that secures our continued independence.

Los Angeles | London | New Delhi | Singapore | Washington DC | Melbourne

Talking of Power

Talking of Power
Early Writings of Bengali Women

Edited by
Malini Bhattacharya
and
Abhijit Sen

Los Angeles | London | New Delhi
Singapore | Washington DC | Melbourne

Copyright © Malini Bhattacharya and Abhijit Sen, School of Women's Studies, Jadavpur University, 2021

All rights reserved. No part of this book may be reproduced or utilized in any form or by any means, electronic or mechanical, including photocopying, recording, or by any information storage or retrieval system, without permission in writing from the publisher.

First published by STREE, an imprint of Bhatkal and Sen, 16 Southern Avenue, Kolkata 700026 in 2003.

This edition published in 2021 by

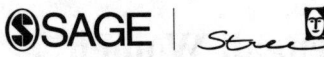

SAGE Publications India Pvt Ltd
B1/I-1 Mohan Cooperative Industrial Area
Mathura Road, New Delhi 110 044, India
www.sagepub.in

STREE
16 Southern Avenue
Kolkata 700 026
www.stree-samyabooks.com

SAGE Publications Inc
2455 Teller Road
Thousand Oaks, California 91320, USA

SAGE Publications Ltd
1 Oliver's Yard, 55 City Road
London EC1Y 1SP, United Kingdom

SAGE Publications Asia-Pacific Pte Ltd
18 Cross Street #10-10/11/12
China Square Central
Singapore 048423

Published by Vivek Mehra for SAGE Publications India Pvt Ltd. Typeset in 11/13pt Bembo by Fidus Design Pvt Ltd, Chandigarh.

Library of Congress Control Number: 2021942959

ISBN: 978-93-81345-81-8 (PB)

SAGE Stree Team: Aritra Paul, Amrita Dutta and Satvinder Kaur Sandhu
Cover Design: Rishi Barua

To the memory of
Vina Mazumdar,
one who gave leadership to the long battle
for women's studies in India

Thank you for choosing a SAGE product!
If you have any comment, observation or feedback,
I would like to personally hear from you.

Please write to me at **contactceo@sagepub.in**

Vivek Mehra, Managing Director and CEO, SAGE India.

Bulk Sales

SAGE India offers special discounts
for purchase of books in bulk.
We also make available special imprints
and excerpts from our books on demand.

For orders and enquiries, write to us at

Marketing Department
SAGE Publications India Pvt Ltd
B1/I-1, Mohan Cooperative Industrial Area
Mathura Road, Post Bag 7
New Delhi 110044, India

E-mail us at **marketing@sagepub.in**

Subscribe to our mailing list
Write to **marketing@sagepub.in**

This book is also available as an e-book.

Contents

Foreword by Tanika Sarkar ... ix
Acknowledgements ... xv

Introduction ... 1
Malini Bhattacharya

1 What Are the Superstitions That Must Be Removed for the Betterment of Our Country? ... 18
Bamasundari Devi

2 The Woeful Plight of Hindu Women ... 27
Kailashbasini Devi

3 A Letter ... 55
Kusumkumari Devi

4 The Modern Age and the Modern Woman ... 59
Saratkumari Chaudhurani

5 A Terrible Problem ... 73
Girindramohini Dasi

6 Independence and Subjugation in Women's Lives ... 81
Krishnabhabini Das

7 How to Establish Amity among the Different Communities in Bengal ... 88
Anindita Devi

8 Women's Dress ... 92
Hemantakumari Chaudhuri

9 What Women Should Do When the Motherland Is in Distress ... 98
Kumudini Mitra

10	The Fruit of the Tree of Knowledge *Kamini Roy*	104
11	The Worship of Women *Begum Rokeya Sakhawat Hossain*	109
12	Proposal: A Women's Arts Association *Hiranmoyee Devi*	121
13	Patriotism *Khairunnissa Khatun*	131
14	On the Use of Footwear by Women in Ancient India *Jagadishwari Devi*	137
15	Words from Times Past *Swarnakumari Devi*	140
16	My Life Changes Track *Sarala Devi Chaudhurani*	160

Index — 175
About the Editors and the Translators — 179

Foreword

Around the middle of the nineteenth century, a social category was born in Bengal, along with a new word that named it: *lekhika* or the female author. Earlier, women's literary compositions had been predominantly oral, eponymous or anonymous, and fragmentary. Literacy, for the upper caste Hindu woman, was considered a forbidden vice, and custom dictated that the educated woman was destined for widowhood. Elite Muslim women, on the other hand, were allowed access to the Arabic Koran, a language which they learnt to read without understanding. When Christian missionaries opened their schools to girls from the 1820s, they could only find low caste children from impoverished homes who could not continue their education beyond the most elementary stages. Parents who sent their daughters to the first girls' school in Calcutta, from the end of the 1840s, were lampooned with savage and obscene comments in the conservative press, and were intimidated and socially ostracized. They had not only educated their girls but also sent them travelling across public spaces to an institution that lay beyond familial and kin-group controls.

More than in schools, women acquired literacy and learning from liberal and radical husbands and fathers. It still remained a very difficult enterprise, fraught with domestic tension. Some of them—like Kailashbasini Devi—learnt their letters secretly at night, after a whole day's domestic labour, behind locked doors and away from the prying, critical eyes of unforgiving in-laws. Her husband insisted that she read and write. Rassundari Devi, however, was entirely self-taught, hiding her secret from a family that was deeply hostile to female education.

Still, women ardently embraced the book and nurtured for it an illicit passion. If the more reformist families encouraged and cherished their educated daughters and if schools and colleges and universities were very gradually persuaded to accommodate girls in all spheres of higher learning—and Indian girls were allowed access to university education and degrees earlier than British women in England—the advance was counterpointed by a hysterical male outburst about the loss of cultural authenticity, of traditional values, of the very essence of Hinduism and Indianness under the onslaught of colonial influence and reformist audacity. The educated woman became some sort of a folk devil: in visual and literary representations, she was someone who had forgotten her mother tongue, her chastity, her body itself had turned masculine, she was someone without shame, hospitality, modesty, concern for others. In this collection, Kamini Roy, as late as 1905, argues against such a stereotype.

What enabled and sustained their transgressive role, and what ensured the transition from the woman who reads to the woman who writes and who is read? If we do not want to replace the Great Men of History model with one about Great Women who transcend all obstacles with sheer individual greatness, we need, perhaps, to attend more closely to the new resources that the emergent public sphere held out. Vidyasagar, as well as missionaries, insisted on vernacularization of primary education, and provided textbooks and primers in a language that was the spoken tongue of women who hardly had the leisure or the environment to master Sanskrit, Arabic, Persian or English in which education was generally conveyed. The simultaneous growth of vernacular prose literature—again with form and syntax that was familiar from everyday use—facilitated learning and especially writing. Print culture cheapened and proliferated reading matter and brought it within easy reach, especially in families which would not otherwise spend much for their women's reading. Newspapers and journals spread news of women's education and some—especially *Bamabodhini Patrika*—cited in this collection, provided not only reading material to the newly literate women, but also encouraged them to write and publish in their pages. Moreover, the entire century resonated with debates on gender relations and ideologies as one controversial marriage law after another was enacted. Muslim reformers, on the other hand, tried to cleanse domestic practice to align men as well as women more closely to the tenets of Islam, and publicized cheap Bangla tracts to project their diverse and conflicted reform programmes.

Given this centrality of gender debates, and given the new resources that disseminated information about them on a wide scale that was unprecedented, women's voices and opinions found a ready market. Even when readers did not agree with what women had to say about gender, they still wanted to know their opinions. In the twentieth century, even if marriage law debates did not vanish from the public horizon, the more serious controversy was, perhaps, about the political role of women, especially in the mass anti-colonial upsurge: what are the pros and cons of accepting their political activism, what should be its preferred form and domain, and where the limits should be imposed. Again, there was widespread curiosity to know what women themselves felt about it. What is very striking is that authors did not necessarily emerge from the ranks of public achievers: those with university degrees, even professions, or public and political roles. Many of the early authors were housewives whose printed writings vaulted across the public-private divide. Their writing went in all directions: prose, poetry, drama, polemic and discursive essays, imaginative fiction. From within their secluded homes—for very few were widely-travelled as Krishnabhabini Das or linked to renowned families and public roles as Swarnakumari Devi and Sarala Devi—they observed the world and confidently judged it. Perhaps, what more successful public achievers could express in their working and public lives, housewives would grasp and construct through writing alone: a new identity, a new relationship with the word and the world.

What they write is surprisingly critical. The present collection spans almost a century of writings. It seems that with the earliest polemical essay of Bamasundari, who happened to be a great influence on the far more celebrated writer Kailashbasini, the Hindu domestic order was unambiguously represented as a site of female suffering, discrimination and subordination. There is little hesitation about relating female unhappiness to prescriptive norms. If Kusumkumari valorizes an ancient Hindu marriage practice, she takes care to select one (Gandharva, or marriage based on mutual desire) that had become deeply transgressive and non-customary in her time. She manipulates this particular tradition to argue mischievously that if this is a valid conjugal form, then the custom of non-consensual marriage must be invalid, and hence a woman married under the latter form was free to undo the tie and marry another man of her choice. Jagadishwari Devi reads monumental and textual evidence from earlier times to demonstrate that women wore shoes in the past. The conclusion subverts and challenges the persistent literary and political valorization in contemporary writings, of the unshod bare feet of the virtuous traditionalist woman as a contrast to the modern woman in foreign footwear. Saratkumari Chaudhurani, on the other hand, does not need to invent tradition; she boldly celebrates the modern. Point by point she deals with the well-furbished male charges against the evil new woman and justifies each of the new ways as infinitely more relevant than past prescription. Again, even when they seem to conform to certain seemingly conservative forms of arguments—tying up women's mobility and education to child-rearing advantages, as Krishnabhabini does—we find that it is a very strategic eugenecism, meant to mobilize acceptance of women's movement beyond domestic confines. It is important to note that by the end of the century, already their demands have transcended literacy and education and now encompass travel and seeing the world. It is also very interesting to find that Krishnabhabini does not use an evolutionary scale to measure civilizational advance: tribal and Englishwomen are bracketed together and are counterposed to the upper caste Hindu women. Similarly, Hemantakumari Chaudhuri castigates Victorian and Muslim courtly apparel as cumbrous and restrictive. If the earlier accent on the educated woman has expanded into a vision of a woman who moves beyond her home freely and easily in lighter and comfortable garments, Hiranmoyee Devi is planning for income-generating possibilities that gesture towards financial self-sufficiency.

There is, increasingly, a remarkable fusion of horizons that denies borders and boundaries between genders and communities.

Kumudini Mitra embraces the Swadeshi nationalism of her father and Khairunnissa Khatun locates new possibilities of freedom for women in the Hindu-dominated anti-Partition movement even though it as yet did not use women in public, active roles. The most interesting effort in this respect is Rokeya Sakhawat Hossain's satirical dramatic skit. It adopts a multiphonal form where a Muslim woman author argues as and with invented Hindu, Muslim and Brahmo characters, each acting as the interlocutor of the other's culture. While every culture is seen to be restrictive for its women, each has distinctive and different ways of doing so. Rokeya quite openly concludes that while all discriminate, Hindu forms are more insidious for here discrimination masks itself as the worship of women. That a Muslim author would express an open critique of Hindu patriarchy is not a sign of a process of Othering that has overtaken women; it is, on the contrary, an acknowledgement of solidarity among all women which enables mutual criticism among cultures.

As women authors find a more assured place in the public domain, and as they are knitted more closely into male literary and political worlds, the earlier strain of cultural introspection and social self-criticism perhaps diminishes. Swarnakumari celebrates older cultural and moral worlds as more hospitable to women than modern ideas of progress and Sarala Devi talks confidently about her multiple successes—political, literary and cultural—in a male-dominated world, without any of the bitterness or astringent criticality of earlier writers. In both respects, there is a partial convergence with male nationalist perspectives and self-articulation. Clearly, the new social category has become heterogenized and pluralized. If a heroic disavowal of norms and prescriptions generated female writing when it was still a deeply contested and transgressive possibility, the expansion of the world of female writers, the points of encounter, and fusion with the male universe—even though these remained rare and available to highly privileged women— opened up shared and intersecting concerns. Mass level anti-colonial movements and their political solidarities provided the major breakthrough in this respect, perhaps, at the cost of a temporary dimming of critiques of patriarchy. On the other hand, the emergence of the political woman and her alliance with male-dominated politics loosened up many of the material constraints of patriarchy, even when they were not explicitly named.

Tanika Sarkar
Retired Professor of History
Jawaharlal Nehru University, New Delhi

Acknowledgements

It is with a great deal of trepidation that we decided to translate women's writings of a period that was crucial for the construction of national identities, whether for good or ill. We felt that the writings might be of interest to readers in the other states of India and abroad, who do not have access to Bangla. We are deeply grateful to the translators who have provided enthusiastic support to the project, and have in spite of their many engagements, complied with our request and taken great pains to complete the work assigned to them on time. We are specially grateful to the Bangiya Sahitya Parishad for allowing us access to their rich archives. Tanika Sarkar, in the midst of her busy schedule, readily agreed to write the Foreword, and we do not know how to thank her. Anindita Bhaduri, Documentation Assistant, School of Women's Studies, worked very hard to prepare the index, and Rumi Mukherjee, also of the School of Women's Studies, worked additional hours to key in the manuscript for us.

Introduction
Malini Bhattacharya

The term 'empowerment' entered feminist discourse in India in the course of the 1990s or so. The Country Paper produced by the Indian government for the Fourth World Conference on Women, Beijing 1995 said:

> The approach of the Eighth Plan which regards women as equal partners in development processes marks a progress from the goal of development to that of empowerment of women.[1]

Thus the term came with the full weight of international publicity and government approval behind it. Its hegemonic role found perfect expression in the declaration of a national women's empowerment policy or of a government-sponsored 'Stree Shakti Varsh' (Women's Empowerment Year) with its array of self-help schemes. Yet it must be admitted that once it was introduced into the discourse of women's movements, it did not remain a comfortable, seamless term representing the panacea for all gender-based inequalities, but became embroiled in debates and controversies and acquired a self-reflexivity that might include explorations into its own historical roots. The term 'empowerment' is now a few decades old; but in order to understand its appeal to participants in the discourse of women's movements in our country, it may be useful to go back in time. Then we may properly explore its nuances in a postcolonial society where the very concept of 'modernity', of which the women's question has always been an important aspect, was subject to the tensions of a multiplicity of intersecting power structures. Colonial power, as well as power based on class and caste, has in such a society modified the lineaments of patriarchal power and influenced the construction of modern gender relationships.

'Empowerment' points to the fact that social formations are also power formations, that they subsist on different kinds of unevenness in the distribution of power, and that this unevenness restricts active agency in social change of large sections of people. In so far as it involves the unpacking of such formations which are generally regarded as wielding unquestionable authority, 'empowerment' is a critical enterprise. However, its exclusive emphasis on 'power' as the basis of social relationships tends to restrict change in such a way that the balance of power in society might remain the same and 'empowerment' could centre on the question of who succeeds in entering the magic circle and who remains outside. In other words, it may relate to the change in the status of individuals and postpone structural change. This may even lead to a position where status quo is maintained in sectoral identities, that is, class-based, caste-based or community-based identities, and a tendency to collapse 'empowerment' with the intensification of some sectoral identities may emerge. Thus the trident-wielding Mother Goddess becomes, at some historical moments, a potent emblem of the 'empowered' high caste Hindu woman. 'Empowerment' as an individual's upward mobility within the existing social-political framework may be then seen as having a particular appeal for classes or groups whose interests are identified with the status quo but who in some way have become conscious of a higher degree of entitlement within the existing structure of power and therefore demand readjustment of rights and privileges. It may be observed that even today when empowerment has assumed a much broader significance, and refers to the possibility of 'equal partnership' in social development cutting across classes, an implicit query that it still contains is: who 'empowers', that is, gives power to whom, and this again brings up questions regarding how the 'giving of power' is perceived by those who possess it. In the context of gender relationships in Bengal in the mid-nineteenth and early twentieth centuries, we may assume that the pressure to move towards a modern, democratic society may make patriarchal 'givers' of power willing participants in the process of empowering women from the same class background, but there may still be a mismatch between the degree and kind of social sanction on the one hand and the experiential reality faced by these women on the other. This mismatch might necessitate modifications in the structure of gender relationships beyond what was envisaged by the 'givers of power'.

In this anthology of translated articles written in the mid-nineteenth and early twentieth centuries by women from the urban elite classes in Bengal, long before the term 'empowerment' came to be used in this context, we have sought to gather traces of such tensions arising out of the need for readjustment in the structures of gender relationships as power relationships. We are, in other words, trying to find out a pre-history of the concept of 'empowerment'. These articles traverse a whole range of nuances from an acute consciousness of women's social powerlessness which gets intertwined with the idea of the powerlessness of the colonized, to the question of 'modernity' and its importance as giving access to social power.

It is not as if 'power' is envisaged as having the same meaning for men and women even when they belong to the same class; particularly in the earlier writings, the 'home' is still perceived as the proper domain for women and it is only the women of the later generations who take up the issue of women's participation in the public domain. Yet it may be perceived that in most cases, power is sought not merely to maintain a companionate presence within 'a new patriarchy'.[2] While it is perfectly true that patriarchy does change its face with the emergence of the nationalist consciousness, women do not necessarily submit passively to its revised contingencies. The women's question, in other words, is not 'resolved' within the nationalist discourse, rather the presence of the literate, articulate, elite woman within this discourse creates new tensions in the texture of gender relationships even if this issue finds no priority in the nationalist political agenda. We find examples of such resistance offered by women's emerging subjectivity in quite a few of the writings in this anthology. 'Power' is sought not merely to serve the revised needs of the family and the home, but for self-development and self-expression; it is a conceptual tool which allows the woman to critique effectively the various inequities of her social condition.

In the literature of social reform of the 1820s and 1830s, the women's condition in colonial India was a contentious issue, but women's voices were then consigned to the domain of silence. Their presence in history could only be guessed from indirect evidence. The education of women was slow to make headway among the urban elite classes, as the statistics of admission to Bethune School in its early years show. Women from other classes/castes who got some education from missionary and other schools may have gone into various vocations but we rarely get instances of these women as readers or writers. In the second half of the nineteenth century, with the spread of literacy among women of the elite classes, however, the silence is breached, and women emerge as readers and writers in their own rights. *Bamabodhini Patrika*, which contains much early evidence of writings by women, first came out in 1863 and we know from Rassundari Devi's own evidence that her autobiography, *Amar Jiban*, the first full-length autobiography to be printed in Bangla, was completed in 1868 and published in the same year (although the earliest edition so far discovered belongs to 1875). If we then take the 1860s as a kind of a watershed, with women beginning to participate in literate culture, a fairly large number of writings by women may be found between this time and the beginning of the twentieth century in various journals and magazines of the period. Some of the pieces were also independent publications. These are the major sources we have used, except for the piece by Sarala Devi Chaudhurani, which is an extract from her autobiography, *Jeebaner Jharapata,* which was published much later, in 1944–1945, serially in the Bangla literary journal *Desh*, and as a book by Sahitya Samsad in 1957. We have still included this particular extract because it refers back to the earlier period and relates very closely with our central theme, namely, the construction of certain ideas of women's power (16, 'My Life Changes Track'). We have arranged the pieces chronologically, as they were published.

In the earlier part of the nineteenth century, Rammohan Roy had made the radically modern assertion that women were not intellectually inferior to men, but that through proper education they might prove themselves to be capable, like men, of acquiring the highest knowledge:

> It is very certain that all mankind, whether male or female, is endowed with a mixture of passions; but by study of the *Shastras* and frequenting the society of respectable persons, these passions may be gradually subdued and the capability of enjoying an exalted state may be attained.[3]

While it seems evident that Rammohan is talking of a conservative, 'Shastric' education and not the modern, Western knowledge-based education that he advocated in 1823 before the General Committee of Public Instruction, what is modern about this statement is not just its gender-sensitive character, but also its perception of self-development, rather than any narrow instrumental end, as the highest goal of education. In spite of this, in the subsequent decades when schemes were drawn up for women's education, in the face of strong opposition from the conservatives, contingency was often offered as the main argument in its support. The piece by Bamasundari Devi in this anthology, for example, asserts that the end of women's education is 'good domestic management, proper behaviour with relatives and the rearing and educating of children' (1, 'What Are the Superstitions That Must Be Removed for the Sake of the Betterment of Our Country').

However, quite a few of the younger writers like Girindramohini Dasi (5, 'A Terrible Problem'), Krishnabhabini Das (6, 'Independence and Subjugation in Women's Lives') and Kamini Roy (10, 'The Fruit of the Tree of Knowledge') add quite a different dimension to the educational aspirations of women; they uphold education or rather knowledge as a means of self-fulfilment and even critique the available system of education for failing to inculcate the needed sense of dignity and confidence in women. These examples suggest that the women writers themselves are not impervious to the higher goal of intellectual self-sufficiency, the 'exalted state' of a truly educated mind, attainable to all, irrespective of gender. Education as a route to intellectual independence becomes an important mode of empowerment. In recent feminist discourse it has sometimes been pointed out that the question of women's education becomes inevitably linked in the nineteenth century with the question of female sexuality and control over it, particularly in the case of young widows. The passage from Rammohan's writing just quoted, however, while it does look at education as a means of sublimation, takes a gender-neutral position in the matter. Kusumkumari Devi's letter in *Somprakash* is interesting in so far as it is an early text and one of the very few texts where the question of sexual freedom is broached directly without linking it up with education (3, 'A Letter'). Free choice in marriage, of course, would become an important question as more women come out in the public domain, but in the writings selected for this anthology, the issue finds hardly any articulation.

In Rokeya Sakhawat Hossain's piece (11, 'The Worship of Women'), written interestingly in the conversational format, four educated Bengali women from a similar class background, two of them Muslims, one a Hindu and the fourth from the Brahmo Samaj, are discussing the plight of women in their respective communities. Prabha's claim that in ancient India, Damayanti, Sita and Savitri were treated as Goddesses is countered by Amena who recalls the story of Khana. She 'may be worshipped now, but don't you know how she died? She was killed by having her tongue cut out, the tongue that gave birth to those precepts.' Jamila does not spare the mullahs either, but she points out that at least they do not practise deception in public by saying 'we worship women'. The conversation reveals that Khana's predicament came as a result of the implicit challenge her skill posed to the public status of her husband.

The anxiety about women being punished for entering the male-dominated public domain through education is powerfully communicated through the transference of the Khana myth to a modern context. The subsequent discussions on *abarodh* (seclusion) and its origin acquire a special relevance in the background of this question of a woman using knowledge to access public life.

In the year 1905, when Rokeya wrote this, the Swadeshi movement had started in the wake of the Partition of Bengal. Nationalistic feelings, nurtured by reconstructed visions of India's glorious past, were running high. But this did not prevent Rokeya, herself a deeply patriotic person, from making an ironical assessment of the status that tradition gives to the Indian woman. It may be recalled that names of Gargi, Maitreyee, Khana and Lilavati were being invoked during these years to prove that women in ancient India possessed a high intellectual and spiritual status. Progressives had been using this argument for a long time to assert that in the present too women must not be deprived of the fruits of knowledge. What Rokeya does is to put the whole question in a modern setting. Educated women do not need the sanction of tradition to justify themselves; indeed, the tradition of 'woman-worship' has something false about it.

This wholly secular attitude is characteristic of Rokeya, but many other women authors writing around the same time, even when they come from the Brahmo Samaj and are strongly critical of Hindu superstitions, are nonetheless inexorably attracted by the pristine myth of a glorious Hindu past. This itself is not unrelated to the question of power. As early as 1865, Kailashbasini, writing on 'Hindu Female Education and Its Progress', had put the blame for the decline in women's education and subsequent woes squarely on 'Muslim rule', suggesting that earlier women's status had been higher. This position found wide acceptance, although Girindramohini and Kamini Roy do point out that women were deprived of knowledge at the time when the 'priestly community' had sought to become all-powerful by monopolizing knowledge. At the time of the Swadeshi movement,

Kumudini Mitra (9, 'What Women Should Do When the Motherland Is in Distress') exhorts her countrywomen to join it in the name of the brave and resolute Aryan women of the past who had cut off their long hair to provide bowstrings for their warriors. Throughout the second half of the nineteenth century, one can give quite a few examples from women's writings of such glorification of a reconstructed past. If the sources of women's power lie in this idealized realm, the present must pay heed to that. It becomes an important constituent in educational thought, although this does not mean that syllabi or pedagogy comes to be dominated by the objective of reconstructing the traditional woman. The Mahakali Pathshala was an interesting experiment, but by no means the only model.[4]

The myth of the golden past, however, became a necessary component of the negotiations with modernity that the writers were engaged in. The traditionalist argument, which deplored the fact that women had succumbed to the blandishments of Western fashion, looked upon education as the disruptive element, the vehicle of moral corruption. There are texts galore, both fictional and non-fictional, which highlight the irresponsibility, flightiness, laziness and sexual laxity of educated women. It is interesting to note that it is not so much the learning of the three Rs that is considered to be dangerous. Traditionalists like Radhakanta Deb did in fact make arrangements at home to allow the women in their families to pick up some education. What was considered to be really dangerous was the participation of women in the public system of education. This might expose young girls going to school to the lasciviousness of men in the streets, and they might learn such lasciviousness themselves from Western literature, thus jeopardizing the sanctity of family life. Education as a means for women to step out into the public domain causes concern to the traditionalists. This is why only a few girls from an upper class, upper caste background attended the early schools. When we compare Swarnakumari's description of the 'lady Vaishnavi' who used to visit the Tagore household with her *Shishubodhak* to impart basic literacy, writing skill and religious instruction to the housebound women (15, 'Words from

Times Past'), with Sarala Devi Chaudhurani's decision, a generation later, to attend public lectures on physics at the newly founded Indian Science Association as a part of her education, we can see the extent of the changes that had taken place in the meantime, changes that the traditionalists had been trying to prevent all the while.

A charge levelled against educated women was that they were completely westernized. The public system of education was regarded as westernized, although the syllabi do not corroborate this. Even the teaching of English in the school founded by Bethune was initially dependent on permission granted by the guardians. What was considered to be Western was probably the opportunity obtained by the girls to move into the public domain, apart from the modern subjects that they were supposed to be learning. Some of the women entering the domain of literate culture were self-taught like Rassundari Devi, but the younger ones had benefited from the limited entry granted to them in the public system of education. How did they respond to the charge of westernization?

An interesting insight into this may be found in the discourse on dress codes. At one point, Jagadishwari Devi (14, 'On the Use of Footwear by Women in Ancient India') had to defend the use of footwear by women by referring to practices in ancient India, but to the generation that followed, the question of women's dress becomes important in the context of more women emerging from the *abarodh* (seclusion) into the world outside. Such egress is regarded by the authors as a given; having assumed that women will be going out, Saratkumari Chaudhurani points out that women's dress in traditional Hindu society is not fit for this (4, 'The Modern Age and the Modern Woman'). The modern woman's concern about what she wears on a social occasion, then, is not just a question of 'fashion', or aping the colonizers, but what is regarded as her own sense of decency and propriety. In Saratkumari's discussion or in Hemantakumari's demand for a 'national dress' for women (8, 'Women's Dress'), the anxiety about a proper dress code articulates not only the desire to develop a system of sexual self-censorship to balance the freedom of moving around in a largely male world, but also the moral discomfort about imitation of Western fashion. Kailashbasini Devi, coming slightly earlier, admits that it is better that Bengali women should appear in public in an 'Englishwoman's attire', than that they should step out 'dressed like a court dancer' (2, 'The Woeful Plight of Hindu Women'). Yet she muses: 'Consider how middle class gentry and common householders would fare if women, so attired, turn into *pucca memsahibs'*.

It may be observed that Western education, imparted to women, gets inextricably connected with the question of social power. In the entire discourse of *swadhinata* (freedom), *paradhinata* (subjugation), and women's capacity for free self-development, tropes of gender power get intertwined with tropes of colonial power. The desire to be liberated from the sense of degradation associated with the colonized status becomes a metaphor of the idea of independence from patriarchal oppression. Women authors of the late nineteenth century deliberately conflate the relationship between the colonizers and colonized with inequities in gender relations. When Kamini Roy raises the issue of the biblical God being against human access to knowledge and says that in history one group has always tried to prevent others from gaining knowledge due to the 'age-old fear of losing one's primacy—"Lest they become like us"'—the charge is as much applicable to the British colonizers vis-à-vis the colonized as to native men vis-à-vis their women.

What the woman is in comparison to the man, the colonized is in comparison to the colonizer. While on the one hand, the woman's degraded and dependent status finds its analogue in the debased status of the colonized, the efforts of the colonized, on the other hand, to recover self-esteem and self-reliance, becomes a justification for the woman's quest in the same direction. Girindramohini makes a spirited defence of women's desire for self-reliance as follows:

> Compared to an Englishman's efficiency, fearlessness, and steadiness, a Bengali man appears as a woman. But we cannot draw the conclusion that the Bengali

men were created to serve as Englishmen's clerks all
their lives . . . It is no longer acceptable to claim that
simply because women have performed small domestic
chores, they will never rise above it even after they
have received education (5 'A Terrible Problem').

Krishnabhabini argues that if women (she means, specifically, upper class Bengali Hindu women) are 'weak and cowardly', this may be linked with the 'half-destroyed' subjugated state of their men. Krishnabhabini says, weakness is perpetuated in the race in so far as women, in their role of mothers, influence their progeny; but the question is whether this is regarded as a natural inferiority.

As I have pointed out earlier, the traditionalists regarded weakness, flightiness, laziness and extreme susceptibility to emotions in modern women as a result of 'Western education'. An article in *Bharati* by Akshay Chandra Chaudhuri blames it particularly on the popularity of the English romantic poets who inducted educated Bengali women to the 'strong inebriation of foreign ideals of love':

> Shyami, agitating her bun of hair perched high on her
> head, makes long speeches like Juliet at the time of her
> marriage, and Bami breathing heavily, imitates Ellen,
> by uttering high-faluting words of self-sacrifice . . .[5]

The glorious image of Indian women in a reconstructed past was meant to recall women to their original nature. Kumudini Mitra talks about this. However, the kind of mocking accusation just mentioned does have some influence on women writers. Quite a few of them feel that the modern, educated woman has lost some of the capacities and skills possessed by her more traditional counterparts, or by women from the labouring classes. Thus, Swarnakumari: 'Good health, labour, normal delivery are now counted as fashions of bygone days.' Saratkumari, even while defending the modern woman against the charge brought at her door, admits that she lacks self-reliance, but excuses this supposed fault by pointing out that 'the modern woman has been moulded to suit the taste, manners and needs of the modern Bengali youth'. This recalls Bankimchandra's version of the self-defence of the 'nabina' (the modern woman) in *Bangadarshan*. Krishnabhabini Das also has a similar criticism to make of upper class educated Bengali women, who are compared not only to European women, but to less educated women from other provinces or from other classes. She says that with all their education, these women have become more homebound, dependent and timid.

This image of the modern woman, created by Krishnabhabini, is however distinct from that of the lascivious fool scoffed at by traditionalists. One can understand that in this critique, an alternative view of the uses of women's education is emerging, and education is being regarded as remaining superficial unless it can give women the confidence to step out into the public domain. Weakness then is perceived not as the result of education but of the failure to put it to its proper use. Krishnabhabini talks of a realm of 'infinite rights' and a 'great working space' she expects to open up for the educated woman once she has overcome her inhibitions. Her concern here is, however, almost solely with Bengali Hindu women from the upper classes. She did write a piece in the early 1890s on the 'Uneducated, Poor Woman,' in *Sahitya*.[6] But the Victorian distinction between the 'respectable' and the 'disreputable' poor constitutes the major thrust in it. The 'positive' aspects of poverty, the advantages of living close to nature are emphasized, and education is envisaged as the major requirement in improving their lives, but the disempowerment associated with lower economic status is ignored. Also, the question of freedom from traditional constraints and of recovery from the humiliation of colonial subjugation, that she raises in connection with upper class, educated women, does not arise in her description of poor labouring women. This vision of a 'great working space' for the former and the tensions it embodied, comes up clearly in Sarala Devi's narrative of her search for a vocation.

The elite background from which Sarala came did not require her to take up a vocation; but she used her family credentials to secure a job for herself in far-off Mysore, away from home. Her refusal to commit herself to a marriage at this stage caused considerable flurry within the family. Her grandfather, Debendranath Tagore, proposed that she would not be pressurized to marry, but might symbolically get wedded to a sword if she took a vow of celibacy to dedicate herself to the service of her country. Sarala was sensible enough to refuse this romantic proposal. Her resolute pursuit of a vocation as a matter of free choice and her journey to Mysore for this purpose, certainly gives evidence of her dedication to her own ideas of self-fulfilment.

It seems that it would not be true to say that with the emergence of nationalist consciousness in the last two decades of the nineteenth century, the identification of the woman with the unspoilt seclusion of the home impedes her increasing entry into the public domain. Where such identity between the two was constructed at the level of ideology, it must have been in stark contrast to the greater visibility actually acquired by middle class and upper class women in the world outside at this time. However, if such visibility signifies power, its assessment is embedded in ambivalence, since in moving out the Bengali Hindu woman is seen as trying to assume the status of the women of the colonizing race. The superiority of the latter as part and parcel of the superiority of colonial power is often taken for granted, and yet the possibility of emulation of their superior example by Bengali women evokes discomfort in women's writings not only because it throws a challenge to patriarchy, but also because it is repellent for the emergent nationalist consciousness.

Bamasundari's piece exemplifies unstinted admiration for the dominant race. She praises their great achievements which she perceives as arising out of their freedom from prejudice. She deplores the fact that caste restrictions observed by Hindus make them look down upon English people as untouchable *mlecchas*. It is significant that it is only on this account that caste restrictions are regarded as an evil, and not because of its oppressive character vis-à-vis large sections of Indian people. But while Bamasundari is full of praise for the colonizers in contrast to her own people who are abjectly superstitious, she would probably not have taken kindly to imitation by Hindu women of their Western counterparts. Kailashbasini is very clear on this issue; she considers women's subordination to be generic, it is through divine design that women are subordinated, and full liberation has not been achieved even by European women.

> If one could be liberated by having education and travelling about as one wished, the women of Europe would have inducted themselves long since into high positions in Government, thus enhancing the glory of their nation.

Krishnabhabini Das is one of the younger authors who does not altogether subscribe to this viewpoint. She does not consider the subordinate state to be natural or universal, although she postpones full independence for Bengali women to a future date.

> We have within these 50 or 60 years not become fit to enjoy the kind of independence that English women have acquired through centuries of toil, labour and perseverance.

This ambivalence about modernity as a derivative category remains. However, at the turn of the century, a new dimension is added to this by the agitational nationalism which offers glimpses of another kind of participation for women in the public domain, again inevitably evoking images of power. Earlier, when Girindramohini Dasi had talked of Bengali men striving for a new, less subordinate status under colonial rule, she had visualized them as rising from the position of 'clerks' to those of 'judges and magistrates'. In other words, the objective was a share in governance for the educated, upper class 'native'. Extending the argument to the women from those classes, her younger contemporaries might also claim a share for themselves in the public domain of 'work', like Sarala Devi.

But with the beginning of the Swadeshi upsurge, as the call for boycott of foreign goods gains strength, women authors like

Kumudini Mitra, who are wholeheartedly with the movement, issue a call to women to demonstrate their power by engaging in the struggle. Deeply embedded in the glorious 'Aryan' past (this is the word she uses rather than 'Hindu'), Kumudini's argument outweighs the benefits of contact with the colonial power by emphasizing the need for national dignity and self-reliance. Women are assigned a special role in the recovery of these by the 'small sacrifice' of relinquishing foreign goods. It is interesting to note that while Hindu or even Brahmo women in reconstructing the glorious Indian past often refer to 'Muslim rule' as signifying its end, this schismatic vision does not seem to affect the thinking of Khairunnisa who, enthusiastically supporting the boycott movement in the wake of the partition, recalls the example of kshatriya women making sacrifices for their country (13, 'Patriotism').

It may also be noted that it is not merely from pristine icons of 'Aryanism' that models of power and self-reliance are derived. Sarala Devi mentions that in contrast to Bengali modes of entertainment like the dancing by baijis, she was struck during her visit to Maharashtra by the male prowess exhibited in their gymnastic and athletic recreations. Subsequently, she would try to induct Bengali youth to similar recreational activities. The need for inculcating true 'maleness' in the Bengali man refers back to the sense of loss of power and dignity as a result of political subjection. In the case of women, too, 'power' acquires a moral and spiritual intonation, even as it is perceived as a recovery of traditional being.

The dangers of stereotyping, immanent in the concept of the woman, less tainted by colonial influence, accompanying and inspiring the male in the quest of political power, are evident in the differentials through which the concept of the 'Hindu' or the 'Aryan' is privileged. It cannot be denied that the situation also indicates a possibility of access into a hitherto forbidden part of the public domain—the overtly political—that women would translate into reality in the subsequent decades of the twentieth century. In the piece by Anindita Devi, where the success of the national movement is described as dependent on communal amity, an open, liberal, humanitarian exchange among the different communities is proposed and a social organization to inculcate the idea is envisaged (7, 'How to Establish Amity Among the Different Communities in Bengal'). Women are perceived in this scheme of things not merely as mothers and wives inculcating the idea at the domestic level, but as organizers and trainers themselves. This idea is quite new and the fact that Anindita Devi considers it possible, indicates that while nationalism creates a 'new patriarchy', very narrowly schismatic and consciously class-divided, it also cannot prevent new efforts to break away from the stereotypes created by it and to articulate the further contradictions it generates within gender relationships. Hiranmoyee's article also finds its inspiration in the Swadeshi movement and envisages a socially constructive space which may enable women to find some economic self-reliance (12, 'Proposal: An Arts Association/A Women's Art Association').

The process of hegemonization is by no means a one-way process. It is continually fractured by new demands from those it had expected to co-opt and mobilize in its cause. If the nationalists wished to perceive their women as mothers and sisters (may be even lovers, as it turned out in Rabindranath Tagore's *Ghare Baire*), who must use their pristine power primarily to inspire them to be true 'males' dedicated to the service of the motherland, the internalization of such images by women must have been far from complete; a state of passive reception of intellectual inputs is certainly not what we may deduce from the evidence of the writings in this anthology. On the other hand, the over-arching presence of class hegemony in the construction of images of power and freedom is not to be ignored. It works through a variety of articulations, but seems to be an important determinant of the boundaries of thought.

Notes

1   Country Report. In *Fourth World Conference on Women, Beijing 1995* (Delhi: Government of India, Department of Women and Child Development, Ministry of Human Resource Development): 1.

2 Partha Chatterjee, 'The Nationalist Resolution of the Women's Question.' In *Recasting Women: Essays in Colonial History*, edited by Kumkum Sangari and Sudesh Vaid (Delhi: Kali for Women, 1989): 251.
3 *The English Works of Raja Rammohun Roy*, edited by Kalidas Nag and Debjyoti Barman, vol 3 (Calcutta: Sadharan Brahmo Samaj, 1947).
4 Geraldine Forbes, *Women in Modern India*. The New Cambridge History, vol 4 (Cambridge: Cambridge University Press, 1999): 45, 49–51, 119.
5 Akshay Chandra Chaudhuri, 'Desaja Prachin Kabi o Adhunik Kabi.' *Bharati* (Asvin, 1289 B.S. [1882]): 152–57.
6 Krishnabhabini Das, 'Ashiksheta o Daridra Nari.' *Sahitya* (Poush 1298 B.S., Dec-Jan 1891).

1   Bamasundari Devi

This piece is regarded as one of the earliest written by a woman in modern Bangla prose. Very little is known about Bamasundari Devi. She spent her life in Pabna (today in Bangladesh) and contributed to the cause of social reform through her booklet, which has been translated here, and expresses her strong Brahmo faith. While her extreme concern about retrograde customs such as child marriage and Kulinism find expression in this piece, it may be noted that she takes a very conservative approach regarding women's status in society.

What Are the Superstitions That Must Be Removed for the Betterment of Our Country?

Om Tat Sat (I invoke the One who exists)

The betterment of this country would be possible if the hatred that the majority of the people here feel against Brahmoism is removed.[1] When faith shines brightly all evils that this country suffers from will disappear by themselves. With the spreading light of Brahmoism caste differences and caste hatred will evaporate; the system of marriage will become purer; no one will be able to attribute to the Bengali nation the sins of falsehood, deceit, perjury, betrayal of faith, and so on. If we devote ourselves to religion and to God, good fortune will dawn upon us. Ah! Let this pure faith be enthroned in all our hearts; let all our thoughts, our aspirations, our discourses and our practice follow this ideal. Whether we are by ourselves or in society or in our place of work let it remain constantly with us. O my Brahmo brothers and sisters, everything relating to Brahmoism depends on you. When you shall be clad in the beauty of this religion; when it shall make you transparent and pure both externally and internally; when you shall be able to show honesty in your work, firm perseverance in danger and gratefulness to the giver of all blessings in happiness and prosperity; when in performing God's work you shall not regard labour as *labour;* when you shall not regard grave danger as *danger;* when the pure austerity of your lives shall be a preventive to all excess, when your home shall be the repository of unalloyed peace, and constant love and affection shall be present in your family; then and then only shall you be a living example to all; your lives shall be like scriptures and the strength of Brahmoism will disseminate itself all over the country.

So long as our faith in the one God is not complete, instead of gaining in happiness and prosperity we shall gradually move to a state of extinction. Alas! The people in our country suffer from such dreadful illusion that they perceive divinity in material forms and worship them with all kinds of offerings, and even offer bribes to such imaginary deities to rid themselves of whatever misfortunes might befall them. Alas! What vanity is this! How can any welfare take place so long as such illusions are not removed from all minds! No, it is quite impossible. O worthy people of my country! Take the sword of knowledge and with one stroke cut down from the roots the thorn tree of false opinions.

The noble Raja Rammohan Roy had established the Brahmo Society in our country, look what improvements have come to the country as a result of that.[2] If Brahmoism spreads over all places and enters the realm of all our minds, oh! what an inexpressible happiness will then pervade our lives! At this moment all our hopes, all our courage rests on this Brahmo religion; if it declines our country also declines, if it blossoms our country will blossom too. What can erase the shameful vices that exist in Bengali society? How can the roots of superstitions, lack of faith, shame and indiscipline be destroyed? Only through the Brahmo religion. Who can uproot the terrible hatred that persists between castes and between nationalities and transform all castes into one nation and all nationalities into one family? That too can be done by Brahmoism alone.

In this world there is nothing more vicious than hatred and arrogance. Our first duty therefore is to abjure these vices.

Great good might come of the habit of travelling if it can be inculcated among the people of our country. We may then learn about the system of governance in different countries, and also learn many languages. It might benefit us if we acquaint ourselves with the qualities of many wonderful trees that grow in other countries but are not to be found in ours. We may also know to what extent the light of education has spread in other lands than our own. If students can travel to England and sit for examinations there, their prestige and fame may be enhanced. But in our country people have this wholly false superstition about losing one's caste by going to England. The one Lord has blessed some communities so that in them this fear of losing caste has disappeared. Believers in the Brahmo religion as of now do not acknowledge caste divisions. If these campaigners of the new outlook decide to go to England and express that desire, their father, brother and others vent their anger upon them, alas! How much this is to be regretted!

Women's education can benefit the country in many ways. Women of our country are completely ignorant about good domestic management, proper behaviour with relatives and the rearing and educating of children. In our country many women who become pregnant do not take proper care of their health. Instead of doing that which would keep them healthy they indulge in practices which are likely to impair their health. They take food according to their whims without any discrimination, and are most careless in their daily movements. They do not know what harm can befall the child in the womb as a result of these irregularities. Had they known they probably would have desisted from these. During pregnancy some women have an irresistible craving for harmful treats, such as unripe kul [a kind of plum] unripe tamarind, chillies, red and green, and potsherds. It is perhaps for this reason that among our people when the ritual of feeding a pregnant woman with objects of her desire takes place a feast of unripe things is laid out. However, this desire for out-of-the way food is merely the outcome of their imagination.

In this country we have the atrocious custom of allotting the worst part of the house as the labour room. The clothes that the women wear are those which are unfit for others' use, alas! The children who are born come out of one prison only to be incarcerated in another.

Their lack of education also prevents our women from appreciating what good results might ensue if women act according to the bidding of their husbands and if they serve their husbands and try constantly to give them satisfaction.

It is the duty of parents to hand over their daughter to a good husband. Oh! If both husband and wife are educated there is no gainsaying how much pleasure they may have in mutual communication. Adequate examples of this are provided by virtuous educated men who live in the company of wives endowed with many qualities. Everyone should without delay look upon the members of his own household with favour and impart education to them. It is incumbent on women to obey their parents when they are children; when they attain maturity it is necessary for them to serve their husbands and carry out their commands, to look after the household and their in-laws, to excel in cooking and to nurture their children.

No woman should regard any man other than her husband with eyes of desire. Nor should she live with any other man or keep the company of unchaste women.

A wife who is competent in housework, dear to her husband, soft-spoken, modest, bashful, chaste, virtuous, paying homage to the one God, enjoys eternal happiness both in this world and the next. The wife whose praises are not sung by her husband, whose husband is displeased with her, is not a wife at all. On the other hand, the wife who serves her husband gladly and without anger in spite of being continually greeted with her husband's cruel words and wrathful eyes alone succeeds in winning her husband's heart and sharing his religious faith.

A husband may live in the city or in the forest, be chaste or unchaste, fortune's favourite or bereft of riches, he may reside in a palace or a hovel, be virtuous or without virtue, handsome or ill-favoured, it is meet that a woman should always be satisfied with him. O women of my country! Practise learning whenever you can spare time from housework, then you will truly know what a great pleasure it is to serve one's husband.

We are unable to describe in words what harm is being done by the absence of education among women. If a learned, liberal, broad-minded man marries an ignorant, quarrelsome, and mean-minded wife the company of that illiterate spouse can never give him any mental satisfaction. Whatever practices are known to the husband to be vain and harmful are followed by his superstitious wife who considers them to be the very stuff of life. The extreme disharmony between the two causes that which is highly respected by one, to be held in neglect and contempt by the other. Thus these couples endure intolerable suffering all their lives due to lack of knowledge and education. Most wives continually quarrel with family members, and counsel their husbands to relinquish them and live separately. Alas! Brothers who loved each other dearly are separated very soon by their mischievous wives.

This country may benefit infinitely if the evil practice of Kulinism is withdrawn.[3] Kulin brahmins may take as many wives as they wish to. Even octogenarians among them have no difficulty in finding brides. The shrotriyas and bangshajas (who are inferior to the kulins in status) consider themselves fortunate to be able to hand over their daughters to them. A five-year-old child may be handed over to a sixty-year-old groom. It is said that many kulin brahmins go through forty, fifty, sixty, seventy, eighty, even one hundred marriages. Alas! When such a polygamous man dies what numbers of wives fall into widowhood and go through unbearable suffering! Therefore, it is this marriage system which has become the repository of all evil and all kinds of sins. We must admit that acts of adultery and foeticide proceed from it.

Large numbers of kulin maidens have to spend their whole lives in an unmarried state, their guardians having failed to find suitable grooms for them. Alas! Their lives are submerged in the sea of sorrow. Noble men of my country! Wake up from your slumber of error, open your eyes to knowledge and see what great evils are taking place due to the practice of Kulinism.

Good may ensue if the system of re-marriage for child widows becomes accepted in society. O what untold and intolerable anguish has to be endured by these poor, powerless, ill-nourished young widows who are always weeping in their grieving hearts; no one taking pity on them or giving them the treatment that might redress this pain. They receive no redressal even when it is there. The fire within their hearts consumes them constantly. No one is merciful enough even to give them a drop of water which may quench this fire. Even while there is water there is not a drop for them to drink. O One God! Where are you? O Truth! Are you still living? O Virtue! Have you disappeared altogether? A stone might break apart on hearing the sorrows of child widows. Those who are penalized by life imprisonment for some heinous crime at least have the consolation that their suffering is in consequence of their sins. How can child widows console themselves? Women who have their sole support in their husbands weep and wail after being widowed, finding the whole world immersed in darkness as on a new moon night. Yet, alas, what matter of regret! No one feels the slightest mercy even after seeing and hearing such things all around him. O all-good, all-powerful God, look at our country with eyes of pity, the unfortunate plight of this country cannot be tolerated anymore.

The status of our country may improve if the system of child marriage is abolished. Alas! O God, is the influence of this evil custom of our country going to multiply with time? Will it never abate? What tribulations people endure by being married off while still in a state of ignorance! Those who have committed this great sin of child marriage have to spend days and nights in finding bread to maintain their families. They have to endure continuous insults in their daily transactions, cursing themselves every moment on hearing the heart-rending cries of their hungry children, and to tolerate the fiery torment of remorse each time they are looking at the sad faces of their wives. A child produced before the body is fully matured can never be strong and healthy. To marry in one's old age is as much of a sin as child marriage. A child born in one's old age just like a child produced before physiological maturity cannot be strong and healthy. A decrepit seed even if it is planted often fails to germinate; even if it germinates it cannot become a strong seed-yielding plant. Similarly, marriage in old age ends in childlessness; even if a child is born that child remains weak and sickly, and suffers throughout life. Sometimes the child is devoured by death, leaving the parents who are responsible for it disconsolate.

Of all the principal causes of the present state of decline of our country, caste prejudice is the foremost. We cannot imagine any betterment so long as this is not abolished. The Hindus look down upon English people as *mlechhas*. They have to purify their bodies with Ganges water if there is any contact, but the great achievements of these *mlechhas* in recent times remain inaccessible to Hindus even in their dreams. It is strange that we cannot get rid of our arrogance even after experiencing all this. To be arrogant one needs to have some qualities. The people of our country have arrogance even without possessing the qualities. O universal benefactor, saviour and giver of joy! Please look upon us mercifully, then and only then can all evil be uprooted. You are dearer to us than father, brother or friend, so to whom else but to you should we make our appeal for the redressal of our fallen state? This is why I appeal to you. O Greatly Merciful! Relieve our country of its sore distress by raining upon us drops of mercy from your infinite storehouse.

Translated by Malini Bhattacharya

From কি কি কুসংস্কার তিরোহিত হইলে এদেশের শ্রীবৃদ্ধি হইতে পারে,
বৈশাখ, ১৭৮৩ শক, এপ্রিল-মে, ১৮৬১।

Ki Ki Kusamskar Tirohito Hoile Edesher Sreebriddhi Hoite Pare,
Baishakh, 1783 Saka, April-May, 1861.

Notes

1. The word 'Brahmo' derived etymologically from 'Brahma', a term found in the Upanishads, was used first by Rammohan Roy to describe a believer in one divine spirit. 'Brohmo Sabha' or 'Brahmo Samaj' was founded by him on 20 August 1828. Brahmoism critiqued the polytheistic beliefs of traditional Hinduism and took up questions of social reform like abjuration of the caste system, women's education, increasing the minimum age of marriage, and so on. Through the initiative of Debendranath Tagore and Akshay Kumar Dutta the Brahmos rejected belief in the infallibility of the Vedas in 1850. Subsequently the Brahmo Samaj was fragmented as a result of internal differences but their intervention in the social and cultural life of Bengal had a wide and far-reaching influence.

2. Rammohan Roy (1772–1833), pioneering social and religious reformer who was well-versed in Sanskrit, Persian, Arabic as well as English. One of the first writers of modern Bangla prose, he translated the Upanishads into Bangla to disseminate monotheistic belief. This culminated in the foundation of the Brahmo Samaj. His efforts at banning sati succeeded when in 1829 the anti-sati act was promulgated by the British government. He was also a pioneer in modern education, particularly women's education in India.

3. An intricate and complex system of hierarchy among upper caste Bengalis said to have been instituted by Ballal Sen (twelfth century). It was a hierarchical demarcation based on nine qualities that the kulins were supposed to possess, and meant to differentiate and give priority to brahmins and non-brahmins brought over to Bengal from north India over the indigenous brahmins and non brahmins in order to maintain caste purity. It was a system of endogamy and hypergamy where social status was sought through marital alliance with a

supposedly higher and purer rank within the same caste. It was regarded by nineteenth-century reformers as one of the most shameful signs of the decadence of Hindu society, encouraging polygamy, a punishing system of dowry and bride price side by side (some paid dowry to attract the higher status groom; others, especially shrotriyas, sold their daughters to the highest bidder) as well as child marriage; see 2, Kailashbasini Devi, 'The Woeful Plight of Hindu Women', this volume. The shrotriyas were the highest in rank among the kulins, followed by bangshajas. Those who were supposed to have demeaned their caste by marrying beneath them were called bhangas.

2 Kailashbasini Devi

Kailashbasini Devi (1837–?) was the wife of Babu Durgacharan Gupta who helped her to gain some education. She is known for three books: Hindu Mahilaganer Hinabastha *(1863);* Hindu Mahilakuler Bidyabhyash o Tahar Samunnati, *where she talks about the degraded lives of Hindu women; and* Viswasobha, *which contains some verse compositions as well. She is bracketed with Bamasundari Devi as being one of the two women who were the first to write Bangla prose.*

The Woeful Plight of Hindu Women

It is practically common knowledge that the women of our country are in a far sorrier situation than those of other civilized nations; and the root thereof lies in our evil-laden social mores. Enslaved by these, what hateful deeds do our noble sires, full of Hindu religious conceit, carry out; what pride they take in tossing out their daughters at a very tender age to unsuitable grooms so that their lofty family prestige may be preserved. O God the Lord, Exalted Ruler of the world! How long till we are rid of our sorrows? How long till the light of awareness shines forth in the land of Bengal, dispelling dark ignorance? O sisters of Bengal! How long till you bedecked in all virtues make Mother Bengal beauteous?

How women of Bengal are born

Thus the expectant mother thinks incessantly till the time she gives birth: 'Pray! If only the Good Lord grants me a boy child, how happy

I'll be, how my kin will love me.' But if, as fate may have it, a girl is born, the mother takes a look and sinks into unspeakable gloom—what is more—is often moved to tears, a sign of utter misery, and the kin shows great distress. Beating of drums, worship of brahmins, feeding the poor, doing propitiatory rites, giving away loads of gifts to prolong the son's life-span and conducting sundry sacred customs like sending the barber to carry the good tidings to relatives far and near—all these acts that follow the birth of a boy are omitted when a girl is born; rather, the opposite things follow. Lord have mercy! Are we so low that the times of our birth and death are equivalent? O social mores! Thy powers are indeed hypnotic! Caught in thy thrall, people are enveloped in confounding darkness. Alas! How long till the land of Bengal becomes the home of happiness and these hated mores are ousted altogether. O Ye Good Samaritan sirs! Pray be enterprising and root out this intolerable tyranny.

What the girl child does and how the parents treat her

Let alone send his daughters to school for education, as he does so sincerely for his sons, the father says, on the contrary: 'What business do they have in getting educated? Will they work outside to earn money? Let them be fed and keep house.' Alas, Education! Art thou there just for money, not for knowledge? Those who have no desire for earning money, will they be ever apart from thee and pass their earthly lives in ignorance? Thanks to you, O social mores!

The sire does not educate his daughters, so they engage themselves wholly in illusory pleasures and pointless games. They spend almost their entire childhood with pots, dolls, rags, dirt, leaves, vines, and so on. Pity! A matter of regret, indeed, that well-wishers like their parents and brothers have totally deprived these tender-hearted girls of the joys of education. Do they not spare even a stray thought on what lies ahead for these girls or how equipped they are to sustain life's journey? The patriarch has no sane counsel for his daughter as to how she, when at her in-laws' after marriage, should behave with her husband and his kin, nor any on infant care. Alas! If girls could have education and parental guidance—they would not then have to suffer so. O Mother

Bengal! When will these miserable daughters of thine be replete with learning and virtue, when will this inferiority leave them and give way to knowledge, which will light thee up with its glow?

Oh, had our mothers been educated, we would not be in such a sorry state. These unlettered mothers teach their daughters exactly what they were taught themselves. They make their daughters perform various rituals and tell them what good these bring about—the daughters too accept the teachings as the word of God and follow them ever after.

The prestige of the clan

Our king Ballal Sen, of baidya descent, conferred prestige and title to the commoners of this country; the self-same prestige has now become a matter of national dishonour.[1] Whether desiring to immortalize his name or to conform to the prevailing practice of the Bengali people, he distinguished the kulins from the mouliks.[2] This, however, has led to much harm. Quite a few among the kulin offspring declare thus: 'Our God-given stature and respectability are quite enough for us. What use do we have for education? The homes we once visit become hallowed beyond measure.' Bloated with such self-importance, they express the utmost hatred for the mouliks, who in turn worship them as Gods. If a kulin visits a moulik on some work, the moulik is flattered no end. Oh, how unjust! Even though the moulik may possess every desirable quality, he gets less respect than a true-blue kulin and, if a father, finds it terribly difficult to marry off his children.

Compared to the middle class and the poor home-earners, however, the rich have less trouble in this regard since they are able to overwhelm all with large dispensations of money. To accomplish the same task, the poor and the middle class have to bear untold misery, implore countless people and visit myriad lands. To reach this goal, some even sell off whatever fixed or mobile assets they might have; meanwhile, if the daughter has turned ten or eleven, the parents, in a spate of hurry and without a care for propriety, give her hand to the first person they lay their eyes on. Having thus rid themselves of the burden of a daughter, scarcely less than the burden of parental after-death rites, they proceed on a blissful existence of food and frolic. But unending despair befalls the ones whose daughters are terribly ugly or physically disabled. They take great pains to marry off their daughters and spend huge amounts for the wedding. The groom goes through the nuptial rites and returns home with the dowry and the gifts. The girl stays back ever after at her father's place.

Among these people are some who for want of grooms organize marriage ceremonies with flowers or trees as grooms. Alas! Only they know what good such a marriage begets; and they reply, when queried on the issue, 'A daughter must be married off, or our parents' ancestors on both sides would be consumed in hellfire.' Mercy! Rather than be married so, girls had better be left unmarried, else married to a groom of similar disposition; otherwise such marriages are sheer delusion, no less. O Lord, great and compassionate! When wilt thou have pity on us and destroy these erroneous ways; when will our friends desist from such grossly unfair practices as marrying a daughter to a tree?

As regards family pedigree, all caste groups stand alike; only the brahmins and the kayasthas are special in certain ways, which, therefore, are documented separately.[3] Kayastha gentlemen of high pedigree, aiming to enhance their family status, arrange to marry their eldest sons to daughters of kulins, whom they pay hefty sums as bride price. Lusting for money, the girl's father sells her off. Having thus firmly secured their bonds of pedigree, these newly kulin gentlemen thereafter marry their sons for a second time to daughters of high-pedigree families; deeming such grooms to have godlike sanctity, these families give them their daughters' hands, along with hoards of jewels and ornaments. Pity! How lamentable that they wilfully drain this bitter cup of bigamy and forever endure the extreme agony that results.

How kulin gentlemen treat their children and what their marriage customs are

It would be good if kulin gentlemen do not hanker overly for money and, with due mercy for forthcoming generations, avoid being the prime cause of corrupting the family lineage (O everlasting misery!). Otherwise, terrible suffering awaits their descendants, poisoned by hereditary ills.

Those whose forefathers took care to preserve their individual worth and dignity are called 'naikashya' sons. The naikashya son first marries into a shrotriya family [highest in rank amongst the kulins], then, to preserve family honour, takes a kulin wife too. However, this wife forms no part of the man's family; she stays at her father's home for life, the children of her womb are denied any share of their father's wealth and they spend all their lives at their maternal homes. It is the shrotriya wife who becomes her husband's favourite. And it is the children of *her* womb who inherit his wealth. Goodness! How unjust of the man to wed the girl and make her conceive, yet not provide her and the children with means of sustenance. The children are reared uncaringly and amid great distress; in absence of a guardian, they fail to acquire education and intelligence. This leads to an extreme scarcity of means so, not having other ways out of it, they fall back upon the Ballal Sen hallmark. They marry daughters of an aristocratic stock in exchange of a goodly sum of money—this is called 'corruption of lineage'.

Ah! Is it not a matter of anguish that the young kulins indulge in immediate pleasures at the cost of future good? Alas! As fire brings about its own nemesis, so is it with the kulin progeny. As smoke from fire turns into cloud, which brings forth rain to destroy its own source, so does the kulin gentleman proceed to demolish his own lineage. The lineage is the fire, the kulin wife the smoke and her progeny the cloud; the fire-like lineage is totally devastated by corruption raining down from the cloud-like progeny. Alas! If only he did not wed the woman of kulin birth or, even if he did, brought her home and treated her on a par with the shrotriya wife, cared for, nurtured and educated her children and bequeathed them a part of his wealth; then might these children avoid the terrible danger of corruption of lineage.

The honour of naikashyas who have no sisters has a somewhat subdued glow; those who have, give the sisters away to families superior or equal to theirs in status. The same goes for their daughters. These marriages greatly enhance their glory, and the ones unable to do so are besmirched by the evil of deterioration of lineage. In order to preserve family prestige, these kulin worthies marry off their sisters and daughters to men who are horrendously ugly, blind, hump-backed, lame, dumb, deaf or even dying. Alas! What a cruel act! The unfairness they mete out to their sisters and daughters merely for self-gain is beyond words.

I heard that once, learning that someone of a pedigreed clan was on his deathbed, a naikashya man thought, 'This person comes from a lofty family, of a stature compatible with ours. If he dies, my daughters would have little chance of getting married and, in that case, my sons would lose their honour. Married to this person, however, they would soon be widows. Admittedly, they are kulin girls and it matters little whether they marry or not, or whether they are widowed. Nonetheless, this marriage is imperative since it would preserve my sons' honour.' So deciding, he married his daughters to that dying and affluent groom.

Hark, Ye Good Samaritan sirs! Judge for yourselves how far such incidents differ from a Sikh killing his daughter. Merely this much—he destroys at once, whereas these worthies kill slowly, by inches. Fearful of having a daughter to marry off and thus being looked down upon, the former engages in that heinous deed, while the latter carry out the detestable activities apprehending destruction of the family lineage.

I am reminded of another example in this regard. In a village on the west bank of the river Suratarangini, there lived a similar 'exalted' one with his only sister whom, he had decided, would marry his paternal aunt's stepson. It so happened that the girl fell seriously ill. When the illness had subsided somewhat, his paternal uncle paid them a visit. Whereupon the girl's mother, brother and other relatives pondered thus: 'This girl was so sick that she had hardly any chance of surviving; who knows when she would be at death's door again? No marriage in that case and devastation of family honour! So let us make no delay and marry her to the uncle.' Having conferred thus, they broached the proposal to that eighty-year-old groom. To which he replied with great irritation, 'Do not marry her to me. Why ruin her? Give her hand to my son who, upon my bidding, is on his way here.' But nothing could put them off and they proceeded to marry off the girl to the old man. The girl, once she came of age, started indulging in extremely despicable activities; her mother, brother and such close ones put up with this vice quite comfortably. Thus it went on until the old man's death, which caused a minor holdup in the girl's self-indulgent ways, so she left her brother's home and set up house on the riverbank. I remember having seen this groom in my early childhood days; he was exactly like a coconut-scraper in appearance.

An account of tri-kulin daughters

A tri-kulin daughter is one born of a naikashya girl wedded to a man who has a naikashya father and a naikashya grandfather. Tri-kulin daughters usually stay unmarried. Like the fabled elderly virgins of *Mahabharata,* they are perpetually in the state of maidenhood. If, God willing, these kulin gentlemen come to hear of a groom having an equivalent family status, they take the utmost care in fetching him and, giving up all sense of propriety, grant him the hand of their sister or daughter. The disproportionate difference in age, resulting from such imprudence, is there for all to see and ridicule.

Once I came to know that the kin of a tri-kulin daughter, residing in a small village on the bank of, the Bhagirathi brought for her a groom much advanced in years. The girl refused to marry the aged groom, saying, 'Do not force me to observe the Ekadashi rituals. I will stay unmarried.'[4] However, if you really wish to see me married, marry me to his son.' At this, her near-and-dear ones married off this woman of thirty, not to the old man, but to his twelve-year-old son whom she then led away by his hand. Good readers! Judge for yourselves how ludicrous the act was. Rather than the groom accepting the bride's hand, it is she who takes him off by his hand! Many other similar incidents are common with these people.

A tri-kulin daughter of high pedigree who lived in a village of Hooghly district, was still unmarried at twenty-six. One day she told her mother, 'I shall turn wayward if you do not arrange for my marriage'. 'I cannot possibly do such an audacious thing,' replied her mother. 'Your stepbrothers would berate me roundly and their family honour would be compromised; for scarcely any house can match ours in status. Should I, because of you, let this greatness go to the dogs? And should I, sullied by the vice of trashing this honour, earn infamy in the after-world as a denizen of Hell and in this world as a family-wrecker? Do as you please then.' That was all the mother had to say. Later, when people came to learn about this, a few gentlemen of the village got together and started looking for a groom for the girl. In the end, they gave her away to the grandson of genteel folk coming from a venerable family. The mother used to live at her maternal grandfather's home. Her mother's uncle, much peeved by the whole affair, turned both mother and daughter out of his home. After that, the persons who had arranged the girl's marriage reached her to her husband's place.

Sometime after this incident, the girl's stepbrother arrived from Chittagong, accompanied by a prospective groom and a matchmaker. On seeing them, the mother was in a great predicament and wondered how she would face his queries. 'Mother,' the man asked presently, 'Where is my sister?' 'At her in-laws,' she responded. Instantly, he exploded like a fireball, 'What? My sister? At her in-laws? Who arranged her marriage? Heavens above! Who has wrought this ruin upon me? Who is it that has utterly blighted the jewel, the honour that is as lifeblood to us?' And thus he went on lamenting and striking his forehead, fit to bring tears to the eyes of all who saw or listened. In due course, people tried to console him through various homilies, but he refused to be mollified and kept saying over and over again, 'Please bring me my sister; I shall arrange to marry her once more and preserve the family honour.' Upon which, the others told him that such a thing was impossible—one who was legally married once cannot be given in marriage again. Frustrated, he said, 'Please then write a statement to the effect that she has died; I shall spread word of my sister's death in my neighbourhood.' And they agreed to this proposal.

There are innumerable such miseries these tri-kulin daughters have had to endure. Unending grief befalls the ones who stay unmarried all their lives. Many bring dishonour to the family and taint the family name by taking the way of easy virtue, such misdemeanour then leading to major sins like unwanted pregnancy. Pity! How sad indeed that they take to such misdeeds only because they fail to get married.

On the 'broken' kulins of Bengal

Persons who crush and chew up sacred family honour on their own in this way may be called 'self-nihilists'. Self-nihilists receive limitless esteem; great is their power, like the mythical Ruler of the Three Worlds. They first break their stock by marrying into a well-to-do family of good stature and subsequently wed again a number of times—people are only too happy to offer them their daughters. Two generations of the sons of self-nihilists and three generations of *their* sons, thus the stock remains undamaged up to the fourth, fifth, sixth and seventh generations but withers away thereafter.

The kulins have a great many wives: to them, marriage is a profession. They start marrying when nine or ten years of age and only give up when they die. Like proselytizing gurus, they travel across lands with baggage and servant. Just as the gurus visit their new disciples to impart sacred knowledge and old disciples to collect their yearly dues, these gentlemen too land up at their in-laws of many years to seek their wives' services and at new homes to fix fresh marriages. Each maintains a record book, which lists the number of marriages, showing the name of each wife and the year of marriage. Those having a degree of affluence are not dependent upon their in-laws; they have a higher status, moreover. They do not set foot in the in-laws' home unless given ten or twelve pieces of silver coins as sacred offering. Most of the fathers-in-law, being petty householders, cannot afford such expense to take in the son-in law, so the girls spend their lives in this state with their fathers; some, for want of their husbands' company, indulge in loathsome acts.

Many a noble-hearted kulin meets his wife for the second time only during his son's marriage; this is the moment too when the son first sees his sire. Heavens above! How hateful it is that these people, far from condemning such depravity, take pride in saying,

'Why should we, of kulin birth, feel ashamed of it? Mention one kulin family free of such doings. It has been common enough with our forefathers, so why should it be a slur on us? We kulins are as pure as the Ganges; just as the holy Ganges remains unpolluted even though nauseating stuff like excreta and corpses are dropped into Her, thus it is with us.' Mercy! How insensate they are that they care nothing even if their wives are wantons and their honour remains unsullied even if their sons are bastards. The lack of devout offerings from in-laws, however upsets their applecart of prestige.

This reminds me of the story of a certain kulin householder, living in a village of Krishnanagar district, who once had his son-in-law visiting his house. No one was there but the daughter who, on seeing her husband after a long time, bestirred herself joyfully and welcomed him. The husband asked her, 'Well then, is there something you have for me?' At this his wife replied, 'What do I, a mere woman, receive that I can keep for you? It is the husband who provides for his wife's upkeep and gifts her jewellery and clothes. So tell me what *you* have brought for me?' Hearing these words spoken in jest, the husband left the place without a second thought and even his wife's earnest entreaties could not make him stay. Afterwards, deeply distressed, the woman contemplated thus:

> 'Since marriage, I have never laid my eyes once on my husband and I am almost twenty now. To him, my character is worth no consideration, he only desires money. Surely I shall have him if I ever get hold of some money.' Having reached this conclusion, she ditched her family honour and set up business in the city of Calcutta. Some time later, while she stood at her window looking down the street, she espied her husband and recognized him instantly. Upon which she instructed her maid to bring the brahmin in, which the maid did right away. The brahmin did not realize that it was a prostitute's house, so he entered and accepted her hospitality. Later, in the evening, the woman loaded a silver salver with a large number of coins and placed it before the brahmin. Seeing this,

he was filled with great wonder and exclaimed, 'Who are you? And what makes you so generous to me? Spare me no detail.' To which the woman replied, 'I am Gourmani, daughter to so-and-so family of such-and-such locality.' These words plunged the brahmin into the depths of amazement and, silently ruing his misconduct, he prepared to leave. But the fallen woman proceeded to speak, 'I have let myself into this evil act only because of you. You refuse to cohabit with me unless you are given money, so take this money and keep me company.' At this, the brahmin was overcome by a pall of gloom and pledged that any of his descendants who married more than once would be deemed to have fallen from sanctity. Subsequently, when the brahmin departed for his home, the prostitute, too, spent all her money in good deeds and retired to the holiest of holy lands at Vrindavan.

Good readers! Think for yourselves how the events unfolded in this case—the sole cause was the so-called honour of the kulin dynasty.

What wrongs the kulins of the Rarhi category commit under the influence of this idea of kulin honour! They give away the girls, so dear to their hearts, to some gaunt and withered old man, on whose death the girls encounter a most terrible widowhood. Who does not know how wretched this condition is? As soon as they get hold of a kulin groom, the parents and other relatives, fully aware of what the girls plight would be, sacrifice all of them— the daughter, the sister, the niece—to the same bull. Alas! It was none other than Ballal Sen who started all this. Had he not planted in Bengal the notion of clan-based hierarchy, a veritable poison tree, this land would not have been polluted by the resulting ills— the fruits borne by that tree.

On kulin descendants

Those born in a kulin dynasty but seven or more generations down the line, or those who, lacking foresight, give away their daughters to lesser families, lose their former prestige and respectability. From heaven, they land with a thud onto the earth and, instead of the dominance their forefathers enjoyed, they suffer its very opposite. The forefathers married many women and abhorred them, whereas the descendant spends much and pays obeisance to many for possessing just one woman. They treated their comely and virtuous wives with great scorn, whereas he, let alone get such a wife, gratefully accepts any unsightly specimen; many remain unsuccessful, even after hoarding lucre like honey bees all their lives, and finally breathe their last. Among the descendants some purchase three- or four-year-old girls at a few hundred rupees and kick the bucket before the girls reach twelve or thirteen. Some marry such children and bring home their mothers with them; not a bad arrangement—reaping immediate benefit from the tree even if the fruit gives none. Some sell off all their assets, fixed and mobile, to escape demonhood in future lives. Four or five brothers may have a Pandava-like marriage and the girl may have several unmarried elder brothers-in-law.[5] Quite a few, in a bid to propagate the dynasty, marry off their younger brothers and become bachelor brothers-in-law. Yet others trade off their daughters against their son's secure marriage.

Such marriages lead to untold misery—destruction of caste, loss of wealth, damage to esteem, and so on. Lusting for money, fraudulent matchmakers arrange to marry these sons of brahmins to low-caste girls whom they pass off as brahmin girls. The groom's father does little scrutiny; his joy knows no bounds on seeing that the girl is of age and inexpensive to boot. Later, when the deception is revealed, he finds himself in a sorry state. Greedy for wealth, kulin wives sell their daughters to families of kulin descent, thereby tainting their husbands' lineages. If, after marriage, the girl stays on at her father's, her near kin often puts her through a second marriage, keeping the family honour intact. Some set up a second marriage for want of money; others make a neat sum by giving away the seven- or eight-year-old girl to a groom who is seventy or eighty. The fact that the girl may be suffering from consumption or other illness is concealed and she exchanges hands for a few hundred rupees. In a few months she dies, devastating the ones who took her in.

A few incidents of kulin descendants' marriages come to my mind. I relate them here for the information of all and sundry:

> I heard from someone that, in the village of West Debanandapur, Tribeni, a groom had just taken his seat for the ceremonial acceptance of his bride when she spoke thus: 'Do not marry me to a brahmin as I am of Sadgop stock.'[6] Those present were stunned at this and rewarded the matchmaker with a generous dose of thrashing.
>
> A brahmin in a certain village married his son to a girl of ignoble caste, but was unaware of this for a long time. One day at the brahmin's home, the family inmates were preparing a sacred thread. The daughter-in-law replied, 'Why do you weave the yarn thus? What kind of cloth will it make? My father never weaves that way.' At this, they asked her, 'Are you a weaver's daughter?' whereupon she fell silent. After a thorough investigation, they found that she was indeed born of a weaver.
>
> A brahmin and his paramour defrauded a city householder by introducing themselves as husband and wife, and parading a barber's daughter as their own. The gentleman and his family were ignorant of this for quite a time. At some stage, she was down with a grievous illness, which caused someone in the house to remark, 'Good grief! What parents! It appears that they have sent her to exile. They have not once enquired about her, though she is as ill as could be.' The instant she heard this, the daughter-in-law said, 'My *parents*? Those people? They are brahmins whereas I am born of a barber.' To the people around, these words seemed like delirious blubbering. Later, when the girl had recovered, thorough enquiries revealed that she was indeed a barber's daughter. Nevertheless,

being a pricey buy, she could not be turned out; she stayed in the house like a maid and subsequently gave birth to a number of children. Behold! A mixed breed is spawned. What name does one call it by?

Child marriage

Who does not know that child marriage is the root of immense harm? It is one of the prime reasons for our wretched condition, the stepping-stone to our misfortune. O friends and well-wishers of our land! Before paying heed to any other issue, please first do away with this extremely harmful practice and bring succour to the masses. Ah me! The great anguish of child marriage is a matter of common knowledge. Who does not suffer its consequences? Who, in the land of Bengal, is not incensed about it? Oh! Would it that child marriage did not prevail here, how blissful would this land then be! Whether it be for pleasure of the eyes or whether it be for living happily and comfortably after a good job done, the parents cast their children into terrible and permanent danger by marrying them off when they are yet wholly immature. For a while, such a marriage does look agreeable to the relatives, but is nevertheless completely shattering to the wedded children since they have no say in the matter. Thus, when they grow up and are able to judge right and wrong, they spend their lives in utter misery, enduring each other's merits and demerits. Maybe the husband, overcome by the ills of stupidity and alcohol, causes distress to both families; or the girl falls below her husband's expectations. As a result, far from being mutually affable, each feels intensely hostile towards the other. So it happens that in most homes marital discord makes its appearance.

Ah me! Would that one could have a spouse after one's own heart—boundless good fortune would then result. Pity! How unjust that the act of marriage is authorized only by the parents or some relative! How unfair that while the looks and qualities of the couple get little importance, the real aim is to secure the finest groom or the all-square wife and to link oneself through marriage to a house of superior status, so as to boost one's own social prestige. They send matchmakers far and near in search of a suitable match. The matchmakers, greedy for money, proceed to delude them through falsehood and trickery, which sometimes leads to disaster. By nature, matchmakers are very crafty and are capable of anything by dint of their cunning; they charm both parties effortlessly and create havoc by adulterating the pure with the fake.

Alas! How regrettable that parents, ignoring their children's views, yoke them in that lifelong captivity called marriage, thinking only about their own prestige and glory, not the children's good or harm in the long run. It needs to be said that, even discounting marriage through mutual consent, parents and other close ones could take special interest in personally meeting the boys or the girls, and judging their nature and appearance carefully, so that they might be married to their equals, thereby putting an end to the dastardly practice of matchmaking. Our good fortune would then know no bounds.

As mentioned before, there is little chance of accord on any issue unless the two are comparable in all respects. Of a married couple, if one is noble and the other mean, the one would most probably look down upon the other. If that be so, how would they unite in genuine warmth and true love and how, without that love, would they stay together all their lives? And how would they bear the fearsome torment, locked for life in that terrible prison? In case the husband is inferior to his wife, she suffers endlessly. If the wife is as ravishingly beautiful as a heavenly maiden, but the husband ugly and disfigured, or addicted to intoxicants and prostitutes, untold bad luck awaits her. If the husband is hideous and repulsive in looks, yet principled, intelligent and possessed of all virtues, he emerges even comelier than Cupid, the highest icon of beauty. On the other hand, if the husband is a cut above the wife in all respects, it is the wife who suffers the greater distress; for looks are a woman's strength and it is common knowledge that a plain visage does not make a wife desirable to her husband. A man, even though unsightly, can attain the heights of excellence through learning and knowledge, a feat that is impossible for a woman. Besides, so what if a woman is full of fine traits? She can never be of a comparable status to a man.

In truth! How gratifying would it be had none of these unfair customs prevailed in our land. It is impossible for a man and a woman to find harmony unless they are closely matched—no other way can love take root. The surprising thing, however, is that, although well aware of such untoward situations occurring in every home, parents and the like never desist from this practice. They continue to marry their beloved, darling children to incompatible grooms and brides. Alas! What a matter of regret that parents put their children in wedlock without prior disclosure of their appearance and character. At that time, the bride and the groom have no option but to agree, but as they grow up and are able to sense right and wrong, both suffer much anguish. Some men proceed to take a new wife, thereby plunging the previous one in a sea of lifelong misery. Some, who are imperturbable and full of profound wisdom, make do with unattractive wives; indeed, some noble hearts are even observed to express a special affection towards them. But the woman finds it humiliating and so, instead of being pleased, she is hounded by remorse.

Thus, it is evident at every step that child marriage is the root of much evil. Unless child marriage is prevented, our land will never have happiness and prosperity, marital harmony will never be established and girl children will never escape the harrowing torment of widowhood; child marriage has emerged as one of the main reasons for the backwardness of Bengalis. Some men, having married early, become fathers even before they are sixteen or seventeen and, with no education, are unable to earn; this makes them crave for ways and means of sustaining their families. There are instances of twelve- or thirteen-year-old girls getting in the family way, thereby putting themselves in grave danger. Some leave this world along with the newborn, casting a pall of deep gloom over the families on both sides. Some escape this fate themselves but lose their beloved infants and, at such tender age, are distraught by heart-rending and unbearable sorrow. Indeed! These girls would not be suffering such intense agony, had there been no child marriage. Even the women who are fortunate enough to avoid such ill fate do not find unalloyed happiness. Maybe the new mother contracts post-natal maladies which cause extreme suffering;

or else the infant is very sick and emaciated, adding to the parents' woes. Moreover, the mother, being immature herself and thus incapable of raising a child, goes through immense hardship. So, there remains no doubt that it is sorely necessary to put a stop to child marriage.

O friends, you who are social benefactors and purveyors of learning! Please put all your efforts to destroy this tyranny of child marriage, which hinders everything good and places thorns on the path of learning. So long as this practice prevails, how will you succeed in advancing the education of women? Girls are only nine or ten when they marry and, before they reach eleven or twelve, are sent to their in-laws', where they are engaged in domestic chores; how then would they develop their learning and intelligence? At ten, they are still immature and have little knowledge about any matter. How then, having received education only till that age, would they gain all-round skills and true knowledge of the facets of education? Consequently, efforts at imparting education are bound to fail unless the custom of child marriage is abandoned.

In ancient times, this harmful system of marriage was non-existent in our realm and the women of yore, not deprived, as we are, of the riches of education, did not pass their earthly lives in useless pursuits: this is borne out by ample evidence from our books on mythology and history. In present times too, therefore, great good would result if people took pains to have their daughters educated on various topics and, with due consideration for their appearance and merits, wedded them to their equals. The women, freed from their terrible predicament, would then pass their days in complete happiness. However, our marriage habits can never be the same as those of other countries; our country is warmer, so its inhabitants reach puberty earlier, and the age of marriage must be correspondingly lower. For boys, the right age to marry is twenty and for girls, thirteen or fourteen. At this age, having left childhood for youth, girls are competent to distinguish right from wrong and, having acquired some learning and sundry domestic skills, can avoid excruciating misery at their in-laws'.

A woman's passage to her in-laws' abode; her concurrent feelings and activities

After marriage, women spend some days at their fathers' and then leave for their in-laws' place; this is called *nabadhabagaman* (advent of the newly-wed) or *dwiragaman* (advent of the couple). During the stay at her father's, a girl wishes to pass her time with her dear ones and is upset if she has to leave them for some reason even for a day. Would she then be willing to go to her in-laws' for an extended or a lifelong sojourn? During this time, she dreads hearing about the in-laws' place; this thought continues to smoulder day and night in the young girl's petal-soft heart and dims the attractive lustre on her lotus-like countenance. Pity! Instead of a joyous heart and a smiling face heightening the parents' pleasure, it is just the reverse. Ah! Seeing their beloved daughter's face clouded over, the parents become exceedingly anxious and start worrying about her ability to adjust at her in-laws' and to bear the intense pain of leaving her old home. Seeing her parents' distress, the daughter, in turn, grows increasingly restive. Oh, how painful it is finally for the parents to force the girl to go her in-laws' and then continue to live in great wretchedness. The girl too, desolate at the separation from her kin, spends her lowly existence incarcerated in the inner sanctum of the in-laws' house, like one imprisoned for the crime of theft.

Mercy! The girl is but a child, unlettered in every respect; so she is as bereft of knowledge as a wild animal. Just as animals are trapped from the jungle by guile and force and brought to a human neighbourhood, where they are tamed through various ploys, similar wiles are used to bring the girl to submission. Like an animal, the girl is not subdued easily and behaves in the same way as a caged creature, which, forgoing food and sleep, continues to brood over its old habitat and keeps looking around the cage for a way of escape. Head draped in a veil, she keeps scanning the cage-like house and goes without food or sleep, pining constantly for her parental home and counting her days to be back there. During this time, she develops no affection for any of her in-laws, who are largely unfamiliar to her: after all, can fondness for unknown people come easily? Far from her having any warm feelings for the in-laws, the opposite is rather more likely. Just as a boy greatly resents his school and nurses a strong irritation for those who sent him there, the girl likewise expresses annoyance towards the in-laws and their home, while people at her parental home, being out of sight, grow dearer yet to her heart. Thus, she treats even a minor visitor from her parents' home as an intimate friend but is unable to convey such genuine warmth towards her closest relatives-in-law. What more is there to tell, even the husband—the most beloved one—receives less affection from her than do the birds, animals and trees at her parental home. During this period, the in-laws' palatial residence appears to her as a rocky range, devoid of people but abounding in fierce, marauding animals; articles of attire, ornaments and other exquisite physical embellishment seem to hurt as intensely as an adder's bite; the most delicious food tastes like foul venom; the alluring bed, as delicately soft as a layer of floating cream, feels as painful as a thorny field; even her husband's nectar-sweet words scorch as unbearably as a lightning bolt. On the other hand, she sees splendour in the ghastly hovel of her parental home and finds it far more appealing than any heavenly mansion; discovers deep pleasure in the few accessories she had in her childhood; relishes the meagre, plebian fare at her father's as if it were some ambrosial delicacy; sleeps on the bare floor as though on a tender flower bed. How can the girl, pulled by such contradictory emotions during this time, settle down at her in-laws' home?

Untold distress befalls those of the girls who, born to affluent fathers, are married into middle class households, or, born to middle class fathers, are married into commoner families. Having enjoyed the best of luxuries at their parental homes, they land in deep trouble at their in-laws', where they get to eat the plainest food and wear the barest clothing, and must slog through the daily chores as befits a maid. Also, if perchance the chores get disrupted in any way, the family elders reward them with torrents of abuse. Ah! Who does not know how unbearable it is when sorrow follows happiness.

How Bengalis treat their wives

While on child marriage I have mentioned that unless a woman acquires all-round excellence, she cannot gain a place of esteem at her husband's side. Established though the fact is, there seems to be no easy way for her to reach such an elevated standing and, on that basis, ultimately to attain a state of empathic salvation, which would ensure her a prosperous family life. This is because she receives no guidance at her parents', nor is she made aware of it at the in-laws'; how then does she achieve importance? What knowledge is she supposed to gain, cooped up in the dark inner sanctum and staring at an assortment of pots, pans and bowls? Or mayhap like a plant, she would imbibe natural virtues. Having received no advice, she remains ignorant in all matters and is incapable of evaluating things that she sees or hears, believing impossible things as possible and ending up as a laughing stock of all concerned.

Asked to cite examples of an idiot, one mentions asses and women; sundry jibes on their inborn stupidity and ignorance are bandied about. A woman is supposedly the repository of all evil: her many traits are elaborated in this context. A contradictory approach is taken on all issues; for example, 'Why is a woman known as *"abala"?*[7] Because like an animal, she cannot speak for herself and is dominated by us, as are animals. Thus, there is no difference between a woman and an animal. 'Why pray, is a woman called *"bama"?*[8] For her lop-sided thinking, of course.' Alas! The unspeakable woe! Not only in the current age, but in ancient times too, women were viewed with such enormous respect. Writers of past eras also have showered us with lavish praise; for example, 'Two-fold in eating, four-fold in cunning, six-fold in trading, eight-fold in mating, and so on.'

Love

Oh, how sweet this word is, but regrettably, soft as it sounds, its practice is as hard. Nothing can proceed without love and each expects it from others: a man from his friends and relatives, a wife from her husband. Thus, each hopes to be loved by others, but none cares to practise it sincerely. If no act is possible without love, can there be marital bliss in its absence?

In our realm, a woman ties the conjugal knot at a very tender age, so she cannot be blamed on this point; rather, it is the man who should bear the burden. Only if the husband displays his genuine affection for her and educates her well on a variety of topics, will she, having come of age, be able to observe and recollect her husband's worthy ways and form a bond of unalloyed love. If this happens, she will succeed in undertaking the voyage of married life with supreme contentment, the devotion to her husband being the sacred feet of refuge. If not, would the unlettered woman, burning incessantly in the fire of her husband's misdemeanour, be prepared to walk that supreme path of devotion?

Nuptial love is about to disappear from our land. The vicious poison of conjugal discord has entered every home. True love in a married couple is rarely observed; the partners are vocal about their likes and dislikes of each other's external trappings and embellishment, uncaring towards each other's sentiments and unwilling to voice their own desires. Pity, that when they must stay together for life as one soul and go about the same business, how can true love emerge from a game of hide-and-seek? How indeed can women undertake the holy rites of devotional attachment to their husbands?

O Lord above! How long till the ladies of Bengal rid themselves of highly despicable and malicious feelings? How long till the soil of their minds is consecrated by the holy water of honesty? And till they are able to spend their conjugal lives in utmost bliss, committed and dutiful to their husbands? And till the full moon of their fame rises to brighten up the all corners of the firmament? O Lord of the destitute! Heed thou my mournful words! Save thou the women from this unbearable agony and turn upon them thy glance of compassion.

How Bengali women school themselves

Currently, women in every household have started receiving education; many of them are learning the native language, while some have read short English books like 'New Spelling'. Still, Heaven only knows how far they will succeed in this and to what extent enhance the prosperity of the nation; for most, reading means settling down somewhere quiet with a couple of fancy, entertaining books steeped in cloying verse and perusing these, just as a brahmin priest, innocent of Sanskrit semantics, mouths a religious text. Some find solace for their minds, as fickle as the Goddess of Wealth, by delving into the estimable *Battala* literature that drips with eroticism.[9] Some cleanse their intellect by watching the glamour of theatrical shows; some, with a dash of English and a flash of frills, bring disgrace to the marital casket of vermillion.[10]

Thus, these ladies, feeling self-important and trying to look sedate, expect a degree of deference from the populace. They shy away from authentic knowledge. Not that they are to blame though, since no one ever gave them the right counsel. Through self-education most have picked up a smattering of knowledge, which suffices them. It is not merely the lack of guidance that hinders their education—numerous other hassles too come in the way. The woman who takes up education becomes an eyesore of the entire family and thereby suffers great anguish. The elders constantly fret and fume in an effort to restrain her from this activity; female neighbours target her with a variety of taunts and forbid their daughters from speaking with her. For such reasons as these, no woman can readily set about educating herself.

We have not been able to fathom the underlying causes for such impediments; opinions vary widely on this subject. Some say a woman who receives education is liable to be widowed. According to others, once she gets to taste the joys of learning, she would eschew domestic work. Some noble souls declare that education would so unsettle her mind that, heedless to her husband, she would try to gain independence, write inviting letters to some man of her choice and make him her paramour. Yet others argue thus: 'Having gained the power of intelligence through education, women would start behaving like men, which would devastate our honour and prestige'. Ah me! Widowed on account of education? Can the might of knowledge kill a husband and deprive a woman of the apple of her eye? In truth! The Lord only knows wherefrom this utterance came forth. Probably the tale spread from the instance of Lilavati, daughter of Bhaskaracharya.[11] Be that as it may, what basis is there for the notion that on being educated a woman would turn wanton and shun family duties? Is learning such a vile thing that associating with it makes a woman fall into evil ways? And why should she neglect housework? Would she, on being educated, turn less affectionate towards her husband, children and other kin? And in what way would she be independent? Can we talk of freedom of the Bengali woman, seeing that she falls from honour the moment she steps out of the courtyard?

The freedom of Bengali women

Alas! A misleading turn of phrase indeed! So assert some exalted minds of Bengal. A woman who has education would not wish to stay confined in the inner sanctum, but rather stray around everywhere at her will, like her counterparts in other lands; and, assuming the air of European beauties, would set about conversing with men. Thus, having travelled extensively and seen aplenty, she would try to free herself of the shackles of submission. It is, therefore, in no way logical to educate women.

Ah! These noble folk, brimming with Hindu religious ardour—the logic they cite! What magnetic force resides in learning that would draw a woman out into the world? Also, what evidence is there that women would crave for freedom? Till now, women of no country have achieved freedom; why then would Bengali women seek it?

The disposition and ability the Lord has granted them amply demonstrate that the subordination of women is the will of God; so the *abalas* [weak ones] can never transform themselves into *sabalas* [strong ones] and acquire freedom. If one could be liberated by being educated and travelling about as one wished, the women of Europe would have inducted themselves long since into high positions in the government, thus enhancing the glory of their nation. Women, therefore, will never have freedom. It does not befit a woman to be without a safe haven. No one has any regard for a shelterless woman; so, if there is no freedom, what chances remain that a woman would roam about hither and thither at her will?

However, many among the modern gentlemen of the new order argue that the nation will never prosper unless our women, like those of other countries, are able to move around everywhere. True as this is, they alone know how they propose to get the women out in the open. For, given that our women lose their honour and status and face unanimous censure as soon as they cross the courtyard why would they readily agree to go out to, say, social meetings? And pray, what accoutrement would they suggest for the women on such trips? The splendour of a gathering would increase a hundred-fold if our women go there bedecked and bejewelled as they are used to; for the advent of such women of heavenly magnificence would make the congregation appear exactly as the court of Indra, the king of the Gods. So, while one can never allow women to step out dressed like a court dancer, it should be fairly acceptable if they appear before the populace in an Englishwoman's attire. Yet, consider how middle class gentry and common householders would fare if women, so attired, turn into *pucca memsahibs*.

If a system is to be put into practice, it needs to be applied to the common people or else its power is lost. Even if one popularizes this system, how does one maintain a balance? Since everyone is keen to experience something new, who would keep house and do the cooking and cleaning if both man and woman leave home to savour this experience? One could reply that education would impart immense capability, by virtue of which everyone could earn prodigious amounts of money, thus enabling them to accomplish any task. Ah! Were this to happen by the grace of the Most Benevolent One, it would be a matter of great good; but would the common people attain such capability? It does not seem possible, ever. And what if it does come about? Our people do not like living alone as the Europeans do and so cannot act likewise. They have to live in association with a number of relatives and their earnings do not match those of Europeans. Indeed, even the most powerful among them earn hardly a third of what a European earns. Thus, their wives can never be as enlightened as those of Europeans. However, if it so transpires that these women are equally at ease working with mud and cow dung as well as attending meetings, it would be excellent for us too.

It is true that in ancient times the Hindu woman had a modicum of freedom and could go about everywhere at will. If one opts for those mythological customs, one should go the whole hog; one cannot adopt some and ignore others. However, wrongful practices, then prevalent, cannot be acceptable now. To preserve the family lineage, some people arranged to have sons procreated through the help of others' than the spouses concerned. A woman, even though an object of gratification of four or five males, could be renowned as utterly sacred and among the first to be revered.[12] Yet, no one can act thus now. It follows that nothing is gained by adhering to ancient precepts.

The agony of widowhood

Ah me! No words can describe the intolerable anguish of widowhood. Alas! In the past, unable to bear this deadly pain, women used to follow their departed husbands through the harsh ritual of the sati thereby escaping the torture; but this custom no longer exists. As a result, widows these days, unable to rid themselves of this terrible, heart-rending grief, continue to be consumed in its fiery incandescence.

Ah! Happy indeed is the home where this vile poison of widowhood has not entered; but unfortunately widowhood has penetrated every household like wildfire and the flames of sorrow are incinerating many souls. Pity! Some people, with their sixteen-year-old daughters-in-law engulfed by the fire, see nothing but an all-pervasive void; others, watching the fire consume their darling daughters, beautiful beyond compare, suffer incessantly in an abyss of misery. Alas! Peace lies at the end of all strife, but this turmoil knows no relief. Pity! Who does not feel sorrowful at the sight of a widowed woman? In truth! The kin, that earlier used to be delighted by her charming vivacity, is now sunk in a morass of infinite gloom on seeing her in the widow's garb.

Alas! How regrettable that on being widowed, women renounce everything and adopt a life of extreme austerity. They lose their former radiance and place of honour. No one cares for widows;

just as a hallowed flower pot, when broken, is turned into an urn for ashes, what shame that a widowed woman too faces the same predicament. Engaged in lowly housework, having one meal a day, they eke out their lives in a thoroughly piteous state.

More! On occasion, some wretches even have to crave for the day-end meal and a rag of clothing. Which heart is not moved by compassion as the suffering of Hindu widows comes to mind? Sooth! Even the toughest of hearts fill with pity to see them, on a cruel Ekadashi day in summer, thirst-ravaged and restless as a bush-fowl craving for rain.

Hail Hinduism! Thanks to you and also to the exalted one that created you, it is the widow who knows what fruits this religion has borne. The worthies that preached thus: 'A human being cannot be called so unless he is compassionate, those without compassion are like animals in human shape'—alas! Why do they now act contrariwise? An ascetic life for the widow, deadly punishment for breach of discipline like drinking water on an Ekadashi day and other such stringent decrees—did they introduce all these out of compassion for widows? Alas, a harrowing tale to tell! Perchance some wretch, severely ill, breathes her last on an Ekadashi day; her relatives, powerless to dispense holy water to her mouth for her well-being in the after-world, pour it into her ear instead. Pity! What a heartless act! For one, there is the unquenchable thirst that fever brings, then the dry fast to boot. Oh! God alone knows where lies the great sublimity of this religion. O ye friends that ponder the good of the country! Do take the initiative and come to the rescue of these women. O Good Lord, thou Timeless One! Be thou merciful and, through thy solace, deliver these hapless women from the terrible maelstrom of worldly existence.

Translated by Kumardeb Bose

From হিন্দু মহিলাগণের হীনাবস্থা, কলকাতা, বাবু দুর্গাচরণ গুপ্ত দ্বারা গুপ্ত প্রেস থেকে প্রকাশিত, ১৭৮৫ শক, ১৮৬৩।

Hindu Mahilaganer Hinabastha, Calcutta, published by Baboo Durgacharan Gupta from the Gupta Press, 1785 Saka, 1863.

Notes

1 Ballal Sen belonged to the Sen dynasty of Bengal who ruled in the twelfth and thirteenth centuries. The Sens were Brahma-Kshatriya, deriving their lineage from dynasties in south India. They were patrons of Brahminism and brahminical influence flourished at that time. The baidyas mentioned by the author are like kayasthas, part of the upper echelons of the shudra community, and supposed to be descended from a mixture of castes. Sometimes it is said they are born of a brahmin father and a vaishya mother.

2 See 1, 'What Are the Superstitions That Must Be Removed for the Betterment of Our Country', n2, this volume; mouliks formed 79 groups and were supposed to be the original descendants of non-brahmin shudra inhabitants of Bengal who were thus differentiated from the group of shudras who were invited to Bengal from north India and were therefore supposed to be of higher rank.

3 Kayasthas were non-brahmins who again observed Kulinism. The mouliks were also kayasthas but inferior in rank to the kayastha who had come from north India. They were quite a powerful group and were involved in judicial and administrative work. See also n2.

4 The eleventh day after the new moon and after the full moon, that is, twice a month, when upper caste widows had to fast and observe very rigid customs They fasted without taking even a drop of water. Harrowing tales about child widows falling ill or even dying while observing these customs were cited by reformers agitating against child marriage.

5 Draupadi in the *Mahabharata* was married polyandrously to five brothers. The allusion suggests that among the banshajas there was a dearth of women of the same status within the caste.

6 One of the fourteen caste-groups identified as nabasakh, who ranked beneath brahmins, baidyas and kayasthas but nonetheless they were higher than the so-called untouchables.

7 A female who lacks strength or *bal,* a pun with *abala,* that is, a female who cannot speak, is intended.

8 Placed left, literally.

9 An area in Calcutta which in the early nineteenth century became the publication centre of low-priced literature. Although many eminent publications came out from Battala, its name began to be touted in a pejorative sense as the birthplace of lowbrow sensational literature.

10 The mark of vermillion worn by a married Hindu woman at the parting of her hair indicates her married status and her chastity. Thus the casket of vermillion is the symbol of conjugal loyalty and honour.
11 A brilliant mathematician who may have been born in the middle of the twelfth century A.D, and was said to be the daughter of Bhaskaracharya, one of the most famous astronomers of ancient India. Lilavati is supposed to have been widowed immediately after her marriage. Trained in astronomy and mathematics by her father, she attained great fame for her mathematical calculations. The third part of *Siddhanta-Shiromani* attributed to Bhaskaracharya, is supposed to have been written by her; see also 11, Calcutta, 'The Worship of Women,' this volume.
12 'Daily remembrance of the holy quintet—Ahalya, Draupadi, Kunti, Tara and Mandodari—destroys the deadliest of sins' [this note is in the original text] the allusion is to Draupadi who was married to the five Pandava brothers.

3   Kusumkumari Devi

No information on the author is available. Her identity remains mysterious. All that we know about her is that she wrote this very rebellious letter on marital choice and that it was published in Somprakash.

A Letter

'To the Honourable Editor of *Somprakash* Esquire
A thought in the heart[1] of a girl born in a kulin family.
"Ill fated mothers, all doomed to misery."

Father,

Everything is determined by fate; else why should man and God both be unfair to the fair sex? I know not what mortal sin caused me to be born in this world among the Hindus. At four and a half years I fell into the hands of a sixty-one-year old saintly soul as if into the fell hand of Time itself. I am now nineteen and have a smattering of education. Although my husband is alive, I am at the moment so deprived of food and shelter that I may truly be called a destitute. I pray that you will deign to answer my questions below to provide me a little relief.

1. I am a free autonomous human being. Why, then, should I suffer the consequences of sins committed by my father, mother or other relations? It is the just dispensation of God that if I remain thus unprotected it is I (and not my parents)

who must be responsible and do penance for it. Then why should I incur the wrath of God for the sake of others? Would you advise that I should?

2. Every daughter of a kulin brings shame upon her family. Who is to suffer the retributions for her sin of going astray? Is it our fathers, mothers or maternal relations, husbands, or even we ourselves who are culpable, and to what extent? Should the king himself share some of the guilt of our offence?

3. There is no atonement for voluntary sins. Even if there is it must be awesome. Kulin girls step into sin knowing the consequences full well. But what is the legitimate decree of contrition for one who is not willing to sin? Is it the prescription of eternal abstinence, or any other esoteric practice of yoga? And is it acceptable to our reason and sense of justice that such prescriptions of endless chastity be observed? Is it even the will of God?

4. If one observes with eyes unblinkered by superstition it will surely be obvious that marriage is but the union of two hearts. No matter how subservient to binding laws men are, in their inadequancy of knowledge, no law apart from that which has the sanction of voluntary decision (Gandharva) may validate a marriage.[2] Thus considered, my marriage stands null and void. And if the marriage itself is invalid, the man chosen by my father cannot be my husband; and if he be not my husband after all, why should I not be able to forsake (though not truly forsake) him to accept the hand of a virtuous man of my own choice? Ancient men in their blindness will surely raise objections, but will you not sanctify it?

5. Should I get married thus, or should I call down calumny upon my family? Which way would you ask me to tread? And if it is legally sanctioned that widows may get married again why should it be denied to women as wretched as me?

6. Should I comply with your advice, or act in deference to the wishes of my parents? Should I not keep to the way prescribed by law? Nor do I wish to withdraw filial respect from my parents, but if I happen to transgress divine dispensation at the behest of superstitious parents, shall I be redeemed in the life hereafter?

7. Eight manners of marriage are sanctioned by the customs of our land—Brahma, Daiva, Arya, Prajapatya, Gandharva, Paisacha, Rakshasa and Asura. But it will certainly be apparent to the discerning eye that no marriages excepting those sanctioned by the law of Gandharva union have yielded happy fruits. The history of previous ages bears testimony to this fact. What more proof do we need? So many people are married these days but would you find a single married person in our time who has attained the true blessings that are attributed to matrimony? It is possible that despite the purity of the knowledge and intelligence of your readers it is simply the manner of marriage that has corrupted their hearts, keeps corrupting, or will corrupt as inevitably as sin. Now may I inquire if I, without corrupting my mind and body, or sullying my life in this world and the next, can retain my purity by accepting the hand of a young man whom I have chosen for myself—should I do so? And why should I not?
8. Between man and God—who ought to be feared?
9. The ways of the world and minds of men are strange indeed. There is no predicting towards whom one's heart blossoms in love. That is the natural course of the mind,[3] and it does not stop to consider beauty or merit. True love is not born of fear, or of greed, or self-interest, nor can it be destroyed by any of these.

    Affection is never inspired unless there is a parity of circumstances. Therefore, can I be held culpable that no affection for my husband ever sprang in my breast? And if one's heart does not blossom in love for one other, can it be made to love that man? You and your readers will surely be in love with someone or the other. Was that love born of greed or fear, or was it born of spontaneous desire? Can you or your reader refrain from loving the ones you so care for? Could you love, or go on loving any and everyone that comes your way? And if I love someone selflessly with all my soul am I to blame for it? Why should I not love such a one?
10. Every compassionate person in our time is committed to promoting widow remarriage, resisting polygamy and child

marriage, and uprooting the poison dregs of Kulinism. But what is their prescription, may I ask, for the Shyamis and Ramis of our society?[4] Do they realize that Shyami and Rami have as much heart and soul, flesh and blood, hunger and thirst as do their men? And that they were all created by the same hand of God? My ideas will offend some people no doubt—it is not proper for a woman to speak with such frankness. But again, if I may ask, are those people willing to take our burden upon themselves? The Hindu scriptures permit a husband or wife to divorce the spouse; why should such laws not be revived in our own time? You may rest assured that the world will be flooded with heinous sins if this is not done.

Yours (with much expectation)
19 Agrahayan 1278 (c 6 Dec 1872)'

Translated by Chandrayee Niyogi

From 'পত্র', সোমপ্রকাশ, ১১ পৌষ, ১২৭৮ বঙ্গাব্দ, ২৬ ডিসেম্বর, ১৮৭২।

'Patra', *Somprakash,* 11 Poush, 1278 B.S., c 26 Dec, 1872.

Notes

1 The word 'heart' is used interchangeably with 'mind' to translate the term *mon* which does not have any single English equivalent free of the emotion/intellect dualism connoted in the post-Enlightenment usage of these words.
2 According to the *Puranas* and other ancient Hindu scriptures, the Gandharva form of marriage could be solemnized without any formal ceremony, simply by the mutual desire of the persons involved.
3 See n1.
4 Representing common names for girls, that is, any young woman.

4 Saratkumari Chaudhurani

Saratkumari Chaudhurani (1861–1920) was an accomplished writer whose articles were published in journals like Bharati, Bharati o Balak, Sadhana, Bhandar, Bangadarshan, Manoshi o Marmabani, Dhruba, Sabujpatra *and* Viswa Bharati Patrika. *She was educated at Lahore, at a school run for Bengalis and later at the European School. After her marriage to Akshay Chandra Chaudhuri, a lawyer and a great friend of Jyotirindranath Tagore, and a fellow enthusiast for composing music and songs, she grew close to the Tagore family. Rabindranath called her 'Lahorini' and reviewed the only book published in her lifetime,* Subhabibaha o Anyanya Samajchitra *in* Bangadarshan, *which he declared presented a valuable discussion of social reality.*

The Modern Age and the Modern Woman

We are never completely happy in our present state of existence. Our real pleasure lies in the contemplation of the memories of yesteryears and in imagining the future. Instead of being content with the present we invariably find our respective conditions rather unpleasant. There is neither thorn in the memory of the past, nor fetter in the fantasy of the future. With the passage of time the storms that existed in the past vanish, all that remains is pleasant memory. Every year even as we rejoice in the moonlit autumn nights, the spring breeze or the smell of jasmine in summer we say to ourselves how wonderful were the moonlit nights in the past—it is never the same now. Spring is hardly in the air this season; it feels more like winter. Even the flowers of summer do not smell as sweet—gardeners have plucked the buds to make garlands. When we strolled on the Strand by the Ganges, the breeze was pleasant enough, the waves were charming too—but somehow at that time there was a nagging feeling of being unwell—maybe one should not have exposed oneself to the elements of weather. Now we remember none of that—all that remains is the memory of the riverside—the waves, the soft breeze and the enticing moonlight.

We remember none of the troubles caused by the boat as the waves hit against its sides or the pain caused by headaches—we remember the song of the boatswain, the pleasant rhythmic sound of the oars as they hit the waters. Do unpleasant memories never remain? Yes, they do, but never with the same intensity. Or maybe we humans do not wish to treasure them. When we nurse our dear one on his deathbed we can never imagine living without him. However, the strange thing is that a few days after his passing away the intensity of the bereavement also decreases. We forget the dead, or at least try to. But the pleasant memories are brightly lit in our minds; we derive real pleasure from them. We tend sweet memories with love and care; think of and speak about them. We do not remember the pain the dear one suffered as he lay dying, but turn over and over in our minds the sweet words he spoke.

It is probably because of this natural discontent with the present that a section of Bengali society has become rather dissatisfied with its womenfolk. They have taken to praising the women of yesteryears and blaming modern women. They say that modern women have become pleasure-loving; they do no household work and spend their time in bed reading novels or doing needlepoint. Some say that this continual lying in bed and lack of work has made them so unwell that most of the earnings of the husbands are spent on doctor's fees. Since children are mainly brought up by maids and servants they are not cared for and as a consequence do not have healthy physical or moral growth. Others comment that women nowadays do not respect their elders, their in-laws or husbands, do not look after the needs of guests and are not affectionate mothers. They say all this is the fault of education. The educated woman has become a bibi.[1] Henceforth women should therefore not be educated. Hundred other examples are cited and in conclusion it is said that marriages have become loveless, maternal affection has vanished, and that as a result of all this men's lives have become miserable. Not only is there no peace, comfort or happiness in the family, for which they work so hard to earn money, but also it is an endless source of misery for them. There is no end to wants and demands. The clamour for money, for more money, seems to increase constantly. Evidently the fault lies in educating women. The housewife's demands for fineries, the doctor's fees, wages for the maids, servants and the cook, all these expenses have to be met. However, if we discuss this matter at length then probably the women of our generation may be exonerated from the blame that hapless men seem to be piling on them.

Those who blame the women of today say that earlier there was no system of employing maids or servants—women of the house did the cooking and other household chores themselves. But the modern woman cannot do without them. She will not soil her hands with cow dung or make paan lest it stains her fingers.

It is indeed true that nowadays women have become conscious of hygiene and cleanliness. They do not wish to wipe their fingers stained with the ingredients of paan on their saris or have soot from the utensils and turmeric on their palms. Earlier it was decreed that the cook would have to take a bath and change her clothes before serving food. Whether or not these instructions were followed, women were used to treating their saris as mops. Since women have taken to cleanliness they now have separate cloths to wipe their hands.

Earlier it was customary to massage oil before taking a bath, but now soaps have come into use. Since there is a surfeit of various kinds of soaps in the market—everyone uses them; so do women. But would those lords and masters who make these complaints kindly answer whether it is not they themselves who bring home these toiletries (powder, soap, comb, and so on) to tempt and please their women? If the use of such foreign stuff and imitation of foreign manners were not approved of by the Bengali male would Bengali women ever dare to use them? Moreover, it surely does not follow that he who cannot afford to hire a cook buys food from the market or has to cook himself? Is it not his wife or mother who cooks for him? It is often said that the wife does not care to cook and makes the poor old mother-in-law do the job. But why is that regarded as a crime? In a domestic set-up the mother-in-law or the mother cooks because it is an arrangement that is convenient for all. Usually the mother does not blame her daughter because she has to do the cooking, but the mother-in-law and her relatives never miss an opportunity for directing a barbed comment or two at the poor daughter-in-law.

In our country a majority of the Hindu widows eat only what they themselves have cooked. In such cases cooking for a few more is not a burden. Especially compared to other heavy domestic chores, cooking involves sitting in a particular place and is better suited to the elderly. For the old are not agile. They are also not burdened with little children. Sometimes the mother-in-law does the vegetarian dishes and the daughter-in-law cooks the fish. In case the latter is busy looking after her young ones the mother-in-law would also cook the non-vegetarian items and then change her clothes. It must also be acknowledged that it is with age that women acquire culinary skills. If indeed one were to cook following instructions of a recipe book then it would be difficult to get one's meal even at the end of the day. Hence with the mother-in-law's cooking skills being better than that of the daughter-in-law and also because it makes better sense economically this arrangement is best for the householder. The mother-in-law does not regard cooking for her own son and grandchildren as a burden. Moreover, are the mistresses of those households that can employ cooks ever relieved totally of the task of cooking? They have to prepare the titbits that the husband and the children fancy.

Since maids and servants are easily available in Calcutta most people employ them. This is especially because the status of the Bengali wife is dependent on having at least one maid. In Calcutta the wife is not allowed to step outside the threshold, if a guest arrives in the absence of the husband or the children, she may not even speak to them. Only those who do not have maids or servants know how difficult it is to function without them. In the villages there is never such need. Rural women enjoy a degree of freedom.

Visitors are also largely acquaintances with whom they may communicate, if not directly then in sign language. If need be they may skip out through the backdoor and bring over an older woman or young man of the neighbourhood whom they look upon as an aunt or a nephew. Also getting hold of maids and servants in the village is difficult. Most people are farmers; they work on their own lands and do not go seeking jobs elsewhere. If they have to seek employment then they come to Calcutta because there is no dearth of jobs in the capital. Since maids and servants are easily available in Calcutta and also a necessity, most people employ them according to their means and requirements. If it were easy to find a replacement for a cook when the old one falls ill then why would anyone take the trouble to cook? It is evident that where there is an easy way of getting something done people use it. Now that there are trams on the roads almost everybody rides on them. How many of those who trudged all the way to the temple at Kalighat bother to do so nowadays? One hardly comes across the once familiar sight of large groups of devotees, adorned with the mandatory white garlands around their necks and sindoor on their foreheads, walking back with luggage on their heads and children in their arms. But in the afternoons one would easily come across these groups returning from Kalighat on trams.

With the breakdown of the joint family system the necessity of having maids and servants has increased. Earlier when a female member of the family did the cooking, the others served food to the children. There was a system of serving a special kind of meal to the children. The men used to go out in the morning to supervise work, and returned at noon to have a bath and lunch, which continued till two or three in the afternoon. Usually the cook did not enter the kitchen before ten in the morning. There existed a custom of getting together all the children in the house and doing a sort of picnic where rice and one or two curries were the usual fare. For this it was not necessary to bathe or change one's clothes. Sometimes it did not even involve cooking. Especially in summer the leftover rice from the dinner was served and hence this meal was referred to as *bashi bhat* or *era bhat*. The advantage of the system of joint families was that everyone took turns to do the cooking, and with everyone pitching in, the burden of domestic chores was equally shared. But now that the joint family system has got fractured one has to take care of sickness, ailments, pregnancy and infants all by oneself. Hence it is necessary to have domestic help.

Many a non-interfering lord of the household will argue that one of the chief reasons behind the break-up of the joint families were feuds among women. But quite different sorts of issues are involved in the question of the joint family system and hence it has been left out of the purview of this discussion. It is evident that one of the major reasons for separate households is that as opposed to the earlier times, in the reign of the British, one does not have to make one's will if one intends travelling to Kashi. In other words, travelling has become much easier. The average person can now afford to travel to distant places without spending an excessive amount of money. Hence he takes his wife and children to the city/town where he is employed. Thus it is possible to say that fights among members of the joint family are not the only reasons for people setting up individual establishments. Earlier on, living in the vicinity of one's workplace was difficult even for single working males and no one could afford to have his wife and children stay with him. He could visit his ancestral home only at the end of the week, month or year, depending on the distance that he had to travel. Sometimes people returned home after a stretch of ten or twenty years. The patriarch then took care of several families. The joint family was the need of the times and everyone had to make sacrifices to uphold it. Now all members of the family want to be as close as possible to one another. Travelling back and forth from work has now become easy thanks to the railways. Those whose ancestral homes are in villages near Calcutta realize that if their families are in these villages then there is no need to rent places in the city. They are willing to give the railways the money that they would have had to spend in setting up establishments. The loving care and affection which they get from their families is something for which they are willing to undergo the strain of travelling daily to the cities.

However, it is difficult to believe that maids are employed solely because the women are incapable of work. In the past boys used to leave for the pathshala after breakfast and return home after noon for lunch. Things are different now. Just as the men are in a hurry to have their meals and leave for office by nine in the morning, so are the boys. Just as the school has replaced the pathshala, the boys' demands for attire have also changed. They need uniforms, shoes and umbrellas and many a time they have to absent themselves from schools when they do not have shoes. Earlier, how many boys from middle class homes could afford to wear shoes all the year round? Only on occasions they wore shoes with their formal clothes. Most people took up the professions of their forefathers. Nowadays people of all castes, whether brahmin or kayastha are making a beeline for schools and offices. In all this great hustle and bustle for being on time for school and office where does the housewife get time to do her cooking or serve anyone properly? Is she able to devote her time to cooking properly? Is there time to prepare all the dishes? Fish curry and rice seems to be the maximum anyone can manage to cook. Then too there is hardly time in the morning for fresh produce to be bought from the market and one has to make do with whatever is in the house. Even before the coal stoves can be properly lit everyone begins to clamour for food. The husband demands his meal because he is scared of being marked late at office. The oldest son is an apprentice and is afraid that his name may be struck off. The middle one says it is time for school, if I do not reach early I shall miss the first class. The third says the teacher will beat me. The fourth child clings on to the end of the mother's sari, crying for food, and the youngest one, the infant, lets out a wail for her milk. Who will take care of whom? It is only those who have ever been in such a situation who can understand how difficult it can be.

The modern woman is perfectly suited to her age. For good or for worse is it possible for the woman of today to be like her counterpart of yesteryears? Skills in cooking traditional items like shaker ghanto [a dry spinach dish] or mochar ghanto [a dry green plantain flower dish] is not enough to earn respect. Everyone is interested in whether she has mastered new dishes like meatballs or curry. Plain rice is not acceptable; one has to know how to cook pulao. The ability to draw alpana on wooden boards, to know how to prepare sweets in moulds or to make kantha are not regarded as artistic skills.[2] Truly they are so easy that it is hardly difficult for the modern woman to do all these and more. In the past whenever women had any leisure they would sit down to chat—one hardly needs to elaborate on the nature of the stories: that they were largely gossip can easily be surmised. With quite a few textbooks now published in Bengali and with women having had some education they do not have the inclination to spend their time in idle gossip. Nor do they have to bribe the women in the neighbourhood with delicacies to come and spend time with them. Affluent women regard reading novels or doing needlepoint as better alternatives to being surrounded by their maids and spending time in idle gossip. The modern woman has self-respect and is not willing to share her tale of woes, gossip about the family or husband with all and sundry. She does not like exchanging confidence unless it is with a special or close friend. The women of today do not find it difficult to spend time with their books, their needlework and taking care of their husbands and children. They do not have to give themselves up to gossip. We also find it difficult to believe how women, unless they are very rich, can afford to laze around in bed, even apart from cooking and cleaning there is a host of domestic chores that the housewife has to do. To say that she invites illness by lying in bed is to subject her to calumny.

Surely it is not due to any neglect on the woman's part that the villages are now devastated by malaria. Then there is the question that she is not hospitable to her guests. Are there guests nowadays who need care and attention? In the past it was sometimes necessary to accept the hospitality of neighbours when travelling from one place to another on foot. It was easy to feed one or two unannounced guests from the larder of the joint family. But thanks to the railways one hardly has to go to anyone's doorstep for hospitality. Thus it is the sign of the times that hospitality has vanished with the guests. Does one come across roadside *chatis* or inns in the western part of our country? Earlier there used to be such *chatis* every ten or fifteen miles. There were proprietresses of the inns—surely it is hard to believe that they looked after guests out of goodness of their hearts or because it would pay in the afterlife. Nowadays all kinds of snacks, milk, sweetmeats and fruits are available at the railway stations. Availability of things depends on their necessity. Society will always have things to fulfil its needs. People become important for each other whenever their own needs arise. Even hospitality had its own hidden agenda: that one's guests would become hosts sometime later. Now no one has that need, hence there are no guests, hosts or hospitality.

The modern woman's taste is also very different from that of the woman of the past. Heavy chunky bangles and jewelled waistbands have gone out of fashion. Large bangles worn on occasions do not evoke jealous comment or gaping. 'Mister so and so may go about that way but he evidently has cash stashed away, no wonder he can give his wife a bangle that large', would be whispered to one's female companion in earlier days and inevitably reach the ears of the proud owner of the bangle. But now there would hardly be any occasion for the pleased owner to cast a sideways glance at the person who made this comment with the 'right-you-are' expression.

The woman of today does not regard it as good taste to adorn her naturally beautiful arms with strings of round, triangular or square pieces of gold with fancy names. Similarly they do not take pride in the fact that they possess a Benarasi sari. They find it ridiculous to wear a Benarasi sari in sweltering heat and to proclaim ostentatiously to the maid: 'How can I afford to soil my sari worth one hundred and twenty-five rupees by wearing it only on one occasion!'

The purpose of garments and ornaments is to enhance feminine beauty. What use would these be if instead these succeeded in reducing the charm of the wearer? Gold ornaments these days are finely worked, one gets to notice their designs. That they are not terribly expensive does not reduce their worth. Expensive Benarasi saris these days get moth-eaten in wardrobes. White garments are now in fashion. Only brides are made to wear Benarasi saris. The girl now wears the gorgeous gulbahar sari of Dhaka only on the occasion of her pre-nuptial feast. Simple bordered saris of Dhaka are now in vogue. The modern woman is often wrongly accused of being shameless. Though women may not cover their entire forehead with the end of their saris, very few Bengali women have dispensed with the tradition completely. On the contrary, the modern Bengali woman's attire shows signs of grace and good taste.

Everyone is aware of the fact that an invitation or a feast for the Bengali woman is an immense affair. Even if fifty people are invited, arrangement is made for two hundred. Sometimes, in spite of such excess, the host is put in an embarrassing situation because the guests pack sweets and other foodstuffs to take home with them. Modern women look down upon this custom. This does not mean that the custom has vanished altogether. However, not only women from affluent families but even middle class women now find it beneath their dignity to sit down for a meal and put away the luchi [fried puffed bread] from the plate and fill earthen bowls containing other delicacies to take back home. Needless to say this custom is bad and causes endless trouble. It is distressing for all concerned. It implies that if you were to bring back a palanquin-full of delicacies from someone's son's *annaprasan* [rice-eating ceremony], you would be expected to return the amount with interest at your daughter's wedding. Yet most guests continue to act like this and hostesses feel displeased. It is thanks largely to the refined tastes of modern women that this custom is much less prevalent now. Except the very poor and the needy, very few women care to bring back food from feasts.

There is often a great uproar over the issue of the modern woman's lack of devotion towards her husband. Maybe some hapless man who has been the object of his wife's disrespect sees the world through his own bigoted vision. Tiffs and quarrels between the husband and the wife existed in the past as they do now. In the past women respected, loved and also feared their husbands. Today's woman loves and respects her husband. Terms like feminine 'chit-chat', 'effeminate' and 'henpecked' were in vogue in the past, indicating that men held women in contempt and thus wives were to a large extent scared of them. In the past women would not desist from speaking ill of their husbands behind their backs and would seldom converse freely with them. There would be no intimacy with the husband till very late in their married life.

The modern woman looks upon her husband more as a friend. Since most men have to husband their own households, their wives are often their best advisers because the well-being of the family concerns them both. It is largely for these reasons that the woman of today is not in awe of her husband; moreover, since she is the mistress of the household, the husband receives her constant care and attention. The element of fear is thus largely absent from the wife's love and respect.

It is true that most families are now poverty-stricken. But that is hardly the fault of the women. In the past one could get a maund of rice for two rupees, the price has now risen to four rupees. The fact that needs seem to be increasing is not because women are worse managers but because foodstuffs have now become very expensive. There is not much more that needs to be explicated. A little thoughtful analysis will prove that with the changing times and with the English as our rulers things have changed and are in the process of changing. It is impossible to stop the onslaught of this change. Our new generation is wonderstruck with the English and is trying their best to imitate their manners. But not being totally happy or satisfied with the state of affairs, they have chosen to blame women as the root cause of the disease. Nobody seems to remember that women have always been dependent on men and follow the examples set by them. The modern woman has been moulded to suit the taste, manners and needs of the modern Bengali youth. The modern young man would hardly bear the sight of a woman attired in a coarse red-bordered sari, wearing a nose-ring, thick sindoor in her hair, a large bindi on her forehead, her teeth stained with tobacco, dark lips, wearing anklets and hair pulled back from the forehead in a bun, let alone stoop to consider her as a wife. Men who are bent on finding fault with the modern woman just think of the positive qualities of the women of yesteryears. Nobody ever stops to think whether women are actually guilty of these faults or whether they possess the true feminine gifts to love, care and nurture. Men wield their pens to write whatever crosses their minds and throw calumny on the modern woman.

Indeed, the modern woman cannot be like her traditional counterpart and, even if she were, she would still not win the love and admiration of the man of the new generation. When we see a cottage with its idyllic set-up with a neat well-swept courtyard, creepers weighted down by cucumber and pumpkin and fragrant flowering plants like kamini, bel and jui, we dream about living in it. We shower abuses on the structure made of bricks and mortar that is our house. But if in reality we were to live in the cottage we would start feeling all its discomforts. We would then realize how difficult, indeed impossible, it is for us to live in a cottage in the village. Even now the average middle class women of the villages cook, wash utensils, sweep and swab, boil paddy to make rice and tend the cows. But consider how many men of this class act as cowherds or make fences with bamboo sticks? How many of them would not deem it insulting to wear the traditional hats made of leaves or the rough wooden sandals instead of using an umbrella and wearing shoes? In how many homes, even of the poorest farmer, would one not find a kameez? But the women of these families would not know whether a jacket is a large animal or some foreign foodstuff. If you were to gift your daughter a jacket during the Pujas would it not be natural of her to demand a similar article of wear from her in-laws during Dol [Holi]? And as a mother, would she not throw tantrums to persuade her husband to buy pretty dresses for her daughter?

Many are opposed to the idea of education for girls, but now young girls are being educated. There are schools and pathshalas in most localities. Parents think, 'All right, she will soon go away to her in-laws, if she is literate then she will be able to write to us and not have to depend on others.' Not only that, these days when people come to select brides they are not content with merely asking the girl her name and then letting her be. The reason for asking her name is obviously to ensure that she is not deaf or mute. But now they need to test her intelligence and learning and hence they ask, 'What do you study?' Unless the girl is educated, it is difficult to get her married. Most college and university-educated young men now insist that mere good looks will not do, the bride will have to be educated too. If at the wedding the educated groom realizes that his bride is not literate it makes him very sad indeed. On the night of merrymaking that follows the wedding ceremony, he requests his brothers-in-law and sisters-in-law to teach his bride to read and write. After the girl bride returns home he sends the standard Bangla textbooks to his in-laws and implores that his wife be educated. Since custom does not permit that the girl be sent to school after marriage she is more interested in her dolls than her books. However her mother will not permit this laxity for fear that her son-in-law might take exception. She coaxes her husband: 'Do teach the child something,' or tells her son: 'Why don't you make Sushi sit with her books in the morning and evening?' Sometimes she implores the handful of educated women in the neighbourhood to help educate her daughter. And even before she has mastered the alphabet there are ardent love letters from the husband. That puts everyone in a quandary, the parents begin to lament that they had not educated their daughter. The young women in the neighbourhood insist that a suitable reply be sent and have a good time selecting verses and songs. Only the girl bride hides herself in shame. So we see that if a girl is not educated, then it is difficult to get her married. And with education there is bound to be a change in her thoughts and taste.

I could go on in the same vein but must now stop. Last but not the least we need to remember that the woman of today is suited for the times.

Translated by Swati Ganguly

From 'একাল ও একালের মেয়ে', ভারতী ও বালক, আশ্বিন-কার্তিক-মাঘ, ১২৯৮ বঙ্গাব্দ, অক্টোবর-ডিসেম্বর, ১৮৯১।

'Ekal o Ekaler Meye,' *Bharati o Balak*, Aswin-Kartik-Magh, 1298 B.S., Oct-Dec, 1891.

Notes

1 The term refers to an upper class Muslim woman and was extended in colonial times also to European women. It came to be used in a pejorative sense in Bangla literature of the nineteenth century to indicate imitation of European dress and manners by Indian women.
2 Alpana consists of decorative and ritual designs painted with white rice paste by women on floors and walls of huts or on wooden boards.

   Kantha, a layered covering generally made of old and discarded clothes, is intricately embroidered with thread pulled from the same cloth.

5 Girindramohini Dasi

Girindramohini Dasi (1858–1924) was born in Kolkata and educated in a school run at her home. At ten she was married to Naresh Chandra Dutta of the well-known Bowbazar Duttas; Akshay Kumar Dutta, the eminent scholar and editor of Tattvabodhini Patrika, *was a relative. Her husband's family was known for educating girls and housed the famous Sabitri Library. Her first book was* Janaik Hindu Mahilar Patrabali. *She also wrote poetry* Kabitahar *(1873) and* Asrukana, *which appeared after her husband's death (1874). She translated Kalidasa's* Kumar-Sambhavam *into Bangla. Closely associated with Swarnakumari Devi, she was a contributor to* Bharati, Sahitya, Narayan *among other journals, and she herself edited* Janhabi *for three years. She also wrote a verse drama on Mirabai. Her works have been collected and published:* Girindramohini Dasir Gadya Sangraha *(Kolkata: School of Women's Studies, Jadavpur University, 2001).*

A Terrible Problem

Today there are intense questions and endless debates about whether women are superior or inferior to men. Some men are taking the side of women and some women of men. It seems that fifty years from now, there was little need to talk about womankind. In the last fifty years, just as indigenous literature has had an unprecedented resurgence women also seem to have had a similar turn of fortune. Earlier, it was only whenever anyone wished to compare anything unfavourably that the unfortunate women were mentioned, such as, so and so is inferior even to women. One cannot claim that this mentality has disappeared altogether but the slogans are different on the outside. Be that as it may.

Nowadays newspapers, monthly magazines, meetings, the theatre, the law courts are full of references to women. Whether this churns up nectar or poison, this movement is a positive one for women. They are no longer the invisible birds in the cage of domesticity, they are now trying to fly and find a perch wherever they can.

They are now ready to claim equal rights in schools, colleges, workplaces and warfronts. How and why did this feeling come to women who were demure and powerless, who were hesitant to take the first steps? It is not necessary to judge this here.

Men have become worried, disturbed and afraid about such excesses practised by women. One group says that exposure to the harshness of the workplace will damage soft-bodied women who will lose all their beauty, femininity and soft graces. Women are not constitutionally built to undertake such tasks; doing petty household chores and rearing children are all they are capable of and that is their duty. No major work has been found to have been achieved by women; the few that are visible are not complete. Women can achieve something under the impulse of a temporary emotion, but they are not capable of achieving something on a sustained basis.

The condition under which women now live makes it likely that they will not be able to achieve this. But that they will never be able to do it has no irrefutable proof. Time alone can prove it. Instead of acknowledging the positive effects on men of education, handed down to them through generations, men unjustifiably make the biases with natural law responsible for the inferiority of women in this respect. Whatever may be their prejudice and belief, it does not matter, but the answer to physical force is not through words, but through physical force alone. Women are deficient in that. Men only allow the minimum examples in favour of women's capabilities, and pay no heed to them. But if a multiplicity of examples is the entire asset that men have, why enforce paucity where women are concerned? By the time men have decorated all the pages in history we hope women will have brightened a few more pages in addition.

Compared to an Englishman's efficiency, fearlessness and steadiness a Bengali man appears like a woman. But we cannot draw the conclusion that Bengali men were created to serve as Englishmen's clerks all their lives. Now many of them have gone beyond the clerical jobs and have become judges and magistrates. No one can accept the argument that just because Bengalis were weak to begin with they should persist in their weakness. Similarly, it is no longer acceptable to claim that simply because women have always performed small domestic chores, they will never rise above these even after they have received an education. It becomes clear if we compare the present state of affairs with the one prior to the nineteenth century.

Some people even ask, if women could be men's equals in learning, intelligence and knowledge, why are they not so? The answer to this would be why could not men achieve, right at the beginning, the civilized and developed status they have attained now? Did they have no strength or intelligence then? One cannot get sugar straight from sugarcane; first you get molasses, which become sugar after repeated refinement; in the same way men have been refined through generations of effort and care. No one has taken comparable trouble with women, so they have remained like 'molasses'.

We find that whenever a woman driven by her own nature gives up the dependent, retarded state of a doll, tries to open the eyes of knowledge, and puts a step forward towards the attainment of humanity, male society confronts her with obstruction, hindrance, examples, judgements and other weapons in its arsenal. What does it mean? I ask, is women's existence not their own? Man and woman are both creatures of the world, one is a father, the other is a mother. It is the duty of both to bring up the offspring. If men need freedom and self-reliance—a great deal of knowledge for self-improvement—to enter a profession and a trade for security of life, why do women not need the same? Are they not creatures of the world? Have women been created only to suckle a child and to be a slave to men? No one can say that. No one can deny that self-reliance is necessary for every created being. Therefore everybody must have it. Will women never reach a stage when they will have to bear both paternal burden and maternal responsibility?

Domestic duty is observed jointly by husband and wife. Apart from this each has his or her own responsibility. Let me ask, when inspired by inflated heroism and goaded by large causes, a man leaves his home and a penniless wife, who is surrounded by small children, and is devoid of any education about running a household, does not his going abroad to sacrifice his life in the battlefield destroy, in addition to the domestic ideal, the destitute wife harassed by minor children? Is this how he reaches the apotheosis of his responsibilities as husband, as father? I ask, does not the woman need special skills and self-reliance in order to look after herself and to discharge the duties of a mother? In a society where a destitute woman with minor children does not get even the job of a cook easily, for whom the law does not provide even a penny in a rich father's house, who can dare say that she does not need self-reliance or need to enter the workforce? But you would rather say, 'Fear not, do not worry, we give you the money to buy a rope and pitcher to drown yourself with.'

The proverb goes that words do not moisten chira [dry rice flakes].[1] But our valiant men have always moistened chira with words alone. Their words are sweet sounding, straight and true, but useless in action. They ask that whatever men earn throughout their lives through hard labour, is it not all laid at the foot of the 'queen'? Why, then, does one worry about work for women? The answer shows rank ingratitude! Let us assume that men are generously open-handed with money, that they have no control over it. Women are replete, sitting at home. Among a hundred women, how many are so fortunate? We can say that those who are fortunate and have access to a large income will never leave comfortable beds and will not try to be men's equals by prising the pen to the ear, wearing the hat, just for amusement. But the same rules do not apply to all of them. Please excuse me, the majority have only barbarity heaped on them. Are there any redressals for them?

One needs a little money for running the household, but there is need for the wealth of knowledge and noble learning in order to live one's life fully. If there is a rich woman who has wealth heaped on her head, beneath her feet and around her, but is deprived of the invaluable wealth of knowledge, we will not hesitate to call her poor a hundred times over. The stamp of this noble education is not a degree. Then we would have found all men with degrees to be decked in humanity. The education that gives knowledge without a spiritual core teaches the crookedness of law without justice, the coating of truth without the cementing of character, the foliage of temptation, the tyranny of selfishness, but no loving heart. Such learning we think is not necessary for women, nor do we have any desire that anyone should diligently acquire such education. The education that makes the heart purer, broader and more developed, through which theoretical lore may be obtained and humanity earned, which takes us closer to 'truth, beauty and well-being'—that alone is noble education and genuinely to be coveted. But if women today try to learn some skill or trade because it is necessary for running the household, what is so laughable about it?

It is to be seen in every country that out of a sense of firm self-reliance men have come to have a blind faith, so that they always claim that it is natural for women to depend on menfolk. Unfortunately, they forget that there is very little in it except the partiality of God. The last argument that men have is that it is the dawn of their foolishness that makes women look for self-reliance. One can only say in reply that it is not at all strange that men see the beginning of foolishness alone whenever women come to show signs of opening their eyes and ears to the world! In China men believe that women have no distinct souls. What is then left? Whatever anyone says, women need not feel dampened; intelligence is itself the guide. The heart alone generates a sense of duty; time is the healer of wounds! They should remember that the days when brahmins had become all-powerful by depriving the society of higher learning is now over.

There is an opinion about women's education that it should only include belles lettres, music and painting because that is appropriate for them. There is fear that the soft core of their hearts may get dry and hard through analysis of hard philosophy and science. First, it is clearly a prejudice. Second, how is it then reasonable for men to be trained in literature, music, and so on, even while preserving manly virtues like firmness and hardness? They should not even cross the threshold of music, art, and so forth, they should only be exposed to physical exercise, carpentry, breaking stones or homicide, so that their hardness, both physical and mental, may prosper. However, since no Newton or Shakespeare has been produced among Bengalis, it is probably not very necessary for them that to be educated they would have to discuss poetry or science.

I ask if the soil that nurtures the hardy tree does it not also nurture the soft creeper? Does not the same juice that produces natural hardness in one, maintain the softness in the other? We then fail to understand why women's hearts will harden if they climb the advanced peak of knowledge. We admit that hard labour does damage to bodily beauty and grace and it is important to maintain these for adequate living. But is it not one's duty to take up hard labour for survival or for child rearing? Is there no element in household chores and child rearing that damages health and beauty? If one leaves out a few elite households what do we see in middle class homes? Grinding spices, cooking, wiping and cleaning the house—all this work entails loss of softness and beauty. Then why is it so harmful to give up this servitude to take up jobs as clerks or as teachers?

Supposing work harms beauty, if men and society do not feel deprived through the lack of knowledge, intelligence and complete humanity of women, if they are satisfied with such deprivations, then what is the harm in being deprived of beauty, which is fleeting anyway? If men, on their part, could stand the lack of knowledge, learning power and bear up patiently with disasters of various kinds, then let us hope that they will not be upset by the lack of a little beauty and grace. And if men are women's well-wishers, then why this deception about softness and grace? Is external beauty so valuable? And is it because men are so fond of softness that a fifty-year-old man does not hesitate to make an eight-year-old girl his better half?

Truth demands that we should also say that respect for husbands is no longer showered like flower offerings. It is being extracted as blood is extracted by leeches. We cannot blame women for this. One can show devotion and respect only to those who are worthy of these, otherwise advice to worship bestiality may not be fruitful and may only result in aggravation of national decline and may not become socially productive.

There is no point in getting into fruitless debates about whether women are superior or inferior to men in intelligence and valour. Let domesticity and workplace remain open to both. It is not necessary to prohibit and obstruct anyone from going wherever he or she wants to. They will desist on their own if they find themselves unable to do something and they will understand properly what their own duty is and will fulfil it cheerfully. Then women, at least, will not feel that obstacles to their improvement are inherent.

There is, however, no dearth of excuses to humiliate those who are already down. A new charge against women is that they are not capable of enjoying beauty—they cannot enjoy the beauty of valour. May we ask what other asset do men bring to their homemakers except the beauty of strength? And what is it they offer in exchange of affection and love?

It is true that in their struggle with the world outside, the soft graces like mercy, caring, and so on, do not get properly exercised, and, as a result, men often become hardened. But this does not mean that men's hearts only nurse hardness, that they have no access to mercy, caring and affection. When a naughty boy has to be disciplined, even the mother has to adopt a hard demeanour, but that does not empty the mother's heart of affection. Therefore it is not credible that confrontation with the outside world will deprive the female temperament of affection that is natural to women.

Men say that it is the law of nature that creepers will always take refuge in trees. Women have no objection to be nurtured under the affectionate care of men. But they may totally refuse to be subjugated under the dire rod of punishment of the oppressor. The pleasure of natural exchange can never be equalled by what is forcibly extracted from others. It is natural love and friendship that are genuinely exchanged. It seems to be right that one should be immersed in love rather than in fear; the latter is mere deceit.

One more thing, since child rearing is the bone of contention, no one has seen men being made responsible for child rearing, whether in elite society or in others, and it does not look as if this chore is going to be given to men. Then why do men deny the happiness of sharing knowledge and freedom as if some great loss would ensue from it? The improved condition of women may lead men to enjoy the happiness and hope of unity between equals. It is also a very strange prejudice to think that there will be no domesticity if women acquire the right to work, or that they will separate from men and will have their own kitchens.

O Men, it is not bad advice that you give to women by asking them to wait patiently till such time that they may expect victory. But once bitten, twice shy, is the way the proverb goes. No excess is good. Who knows if it is excessive patience and faith that have made women so dependent that they have come to this present degraded state? What else can happen? We feel that if men use their power in a considerate manner, then this conflict between the stomach and the head will be resolved.[2] Nor will it be necessary any longer for devoted women to turn rebellious or sinful.

Translated by Jasodhara Bagchi

From 'বিষম সমস্যা', ভারতী, শ্রাবণ, ১৩০১ বঙ্গাব্দ, জুলাই-আগস্ট, ১৮৯৪।

'Bisham Samasya', *Bharati, Sravan*, 1301 B.S., July-August, 1894.

Notes

The title reveals a pun in the adjective *bisham*, that is both 'terrible' and 'unequal'.

1   Chira, a favourite snack, is dry and hard and can be eaten after it has been soaked in water. The proverb means that you cannot get very far with empty words.
2   A fable by Aesop which propounds the moral that the stomach and the head, which are parts of the same body, cannot do without each other.

6 Krishnabhabini Das

Krishnabhabini Das (1864–1919) was one of the many women who were educated at home and by their husbands. She was married, aged nine, to Debendranath Das who went to England to study for the civil service examinations. When he returned he was disowned by his father and ostracized by his caste for having broken the caste taboo of travelling abroad. Krishnabhabini accompanied him on his next visit to England despite tremendous family pressure that forced her to leave behind her only child, her daughter, Tilottama. Krishnabhabini lived in England for 14 years. She was much impressed by the emancipation of Englishwomen and wrote about her impressions of England in Englande Bangamahila *(1885).[1] In 1909 she lost both her husband and her daughter and became a member of Bharat Stree Mahamandal that worked for the education of women. She also founded a home for widows. Though without any formal education, she was appointed as examiner by the University of Calcutta. She wrote for distinguished journals like* Bharati o Balak, Sahitya, Pradip *and* Prabasi.

Independence and Subjugation in Women's Lives

As there are great differences between India and England, there are also similar differences between the Indian woman and the Englishwoman. One is weak and cowardly and always looks to someone else for help, while the other is strong, brave and self-dependent. One is like a hindrance to the working life of her husband and son—but the other is a great help to her menfolk.

I shall try as best as I can to find out the reasons for these differences in the lives of these two women.

I used to think education would give us emancipation—we would be brave and self-dependent and able to discriminate critically between good and bad. But now I find that I was wrong. What our mothers and grandmothers were able to do, to tell the good from the bad, is lost to us now. Our daughters in comparison are much more dependent on others, and unable to judge what is good and what is bad, and they have gone a step further down. It cannot be said that this is due to lack of education. The way the women's educational movement has progressed over the last fifty years and the avenues that have opened up for them over the period were totally absent fifty or sixty years ago. Our grandmothers had absolutely no education, our mothers studied only Bangla. Our daughters have learnt even English; despite this their minds are even narrower and the working space in their lives has shrunk further. What could be the reason? Why are the lives of modern Hindu women regressing as compared to their counterparts in the past?

Now I clearly realize and regretfully acknowledge that the first and foremost reason for the backwardness of Hindu women is their complete subjugation and dependence on others. Leave aside the question of Englishwomen, if you consider the situation in India, you will find among the different peoples here the greater the independence the higher is the level of advancement in women's lives. And it is those liberated women who will show greater strength and courage and it is they who will be more self-dependent. It is widely known that among the Parsees 'home-boundedness' is not as rigid as among the Hindus, that is why Parsee women are more courageous and stronger and more self-dependent than their Hindu sisters. Whoever has ever visited Bombay has rejoiced in looking at their vibrant faces and getting to know their hard-working life. In a Parsee home the women are always held in high esteem—the mother, in her absence, the wife, is the real queen of the household—even the male king has no right to dominate over her. The Parsees are continuing the tradition in respect of social customs for hundreds of years. True that their wives and daughters now enjoy greater opportunities of education than before, but that they have not lost their former independence is why they are now in a position to play a greater and more active role in the household.

Look again. The women of the Himalayan provinces like Kashmir, Sikkim and Bhutan are so accomplished, active and independent that it always gives pleasure to any kind-hearted gentleman. They are extremely well dressed, they show cultivated social behaviour—and their presence in the household is even more helpful than the menfolk's. They do not have an iota of formal education, but having enjoyed the same kind of independence as their male counterparts they have become so courageous and lively and active that one cannot help admiring these qualities in them.

In earlier times there was no system of female education here, but the menfolk would have full faith and dependence on them— they like other independent women were the real queens of the households. In matters relating to larger issues women should be expected to act in consultation with their husbands and sons, but in small matters they must be given full independence. Unless you give them to understand that they have responsibilities and that people depend on them, how else would they get used to it? We ourselves have seen with our own eyes that our mothers and grandmothers used to be completely independent in such matters as visiting relatives, taking care of those who fell ill, making arrangements for guests, rendering benevolent services to others and inviting people to their homes. But now the lives of our women have become so limited and dependent upon others that they cannot visit their parents' homes even when their brothers or sisters are ill. Now we derive pleasure reading at home, books written in English and charming stories in Bengali. We also come to know about foreign lands through newspapers. True that we do no longer take our planet earth as 'triangular' or consider earthquakes as due to Basuki changing his shoulders[2] —but Bengali women have not made any real progress in their lives. The bookish knowledge we have had is confined just within the four walls of our homes. If it is necessary that you have to come out of your home—as it was in the earthquake last June—I am afraid that our women now would not be able to protect themselves as adequately as Hindu women could do some fifty years ago. We have heard that our grandmothers would often kill snakes in their store rooms, but now we get scared at the sight of cockroaches, not to speak of killing scorpions! Might we not realize through these instances the importance of an independent life in giving us courage and possibly also other advantages, especially when compared to the cowardliness and other disadvantages in a subjugated life?

Be it any country of the East or of the West or be it any civilized or uncivilized country, I do not think that we can ever find a woman whose life will compare with the endless misfortune of that of the subjugated Bengali woman. Leave aside the women of the cultivated races in Asia, Europe and America, I have compared the lives of the Bengali women with those of women of other Indian provinces and also of some forest-dwelling tribes—and I have found that the lives of Bengali women are simply woeful and miserable. To know the lives of women of any country we usually carefully follow the customs and practices of the ordinary people of that country. If we consider the fathers' behaviour towards their daughters, the sons' regards for their mothers, the kind of relations that normally exists between husbands and wives, the way the brothers are attached to their sisters and how the ordinary menfolk look upon their womenfolk, we may then know about the real happiness and comfort and development of the worldly life of the people. Therefore, while considering the state of independence of the Hindu women we have to first examine their domestic lives.

I am sorry to have to put it down here that barring a few families in most Bengali households the women are generally ill-treated. And on the whole it clearly appears that the condition of the Bengali women is deteriorating day by day. There may be someone who on reading this particular line would exclaim—Oh! It's impossible, these women, they can never be satisfied! Look, our mothers and grandmothers would pass their days applying rancid coconut oil on their hair and relaxing on bare mud floors, and now these ladies spray perfumes on their bodies and their living rooms are now adorned with chairs and sofas, but still they are grumbling that the lives of present-day women are gradually moving from bad to worse! But this is really not a joke and this essay is not being written for one who would suppose real happiness consists in perfumes and comfortable furniture. Can any intelligent thoughtful person deny that in our land the condition of women, on whom depends the future development and stability of the Hindu nation, is gradually worsening? Whenever we visit a family, no matter whether educated or illiterate, we invariably find instances of lack of respect of the son for the mother, the neglect of the father for the daughter, lack of faith of the brothers for the sisters, hatred of the husband for the wife—all these wrongdoings are to be seen everywhere. I do admit that Bengali women are less educated than their male counterparts, but do they deserve to be mistreated for that social evil? Is it what a gentleman or an educated man should do? Barring only a few in America or England, women in no other country are as educated as men. And I have already argued that education alone cannot make one's mind rich and cultivated. Along with education one needs practical knowledge and experience of the outside world; it is only then that human life can become truly cultivated, bold and brave and effectively valuable. But when the way to real knowledge is closed, how can the women be expected to be courageous, strong and self-reliant?

One may argue that the liberation of women is now a reality among the Brahmos, but still that does not seem to produce good results. Those who do not know the value of independence had better be kept under others' domination, though it seems that when our Brahmo brothers have become particularly careful about women's emancipation and are eager that their wives and daughters should enjoy its benefits we are certain to get the results sooner or later. But at the same time we should keep it in mind that we have within this span of fifty or sixty years not become fit to enjoy the kind of independence that the Englishwomen have acquired through centuries of toil, labour and perseverance. Men do not learn to walk in a day, the birds cannot fly at one go. Before they can walk or fly their mothers, as any intelligent person would know, have to take a good deal of care to tend the children and the birdies to stand on their own feet or to spread their wings. Likewise let the Hindu women be allowed to go about in the world after being tended to deserve independence, and you will see that they will not fail to prove themselves worthy. They will find their proper place in this worldly life and will keep themselves steadfast to protect their home and family and will be teachers to their children and able to assist their husbands and sons.

As they have been confined at home for a long period, it is not the women alone that are weak and cowardly and insipid in India. We find that the root cause of the half-destroyed life of the Hindu also lies in this subjugation. One must have noticed that the Hindus are gradually becoming more and more weak and cowardly. They show no strength of physique, nor any joy of life, nor do they have any enthusiasm in their action. They show a lack of faith in all their work and a pervading element of negligence in every sphere. How long can we really sustain this struggle in an atmosphere of timid sterility?

We find in this subjugation of the Hindu women the root cause of the rather low expectancy of life of the people of this country. We learn from the statistics of birth and death that half the children born here are dead by the time they are five years old. What a great tragedy! As a beautiful rose cutting withers away when planted in an uncongenial soil, the child-flower similarly dries up, feeding on the unhealthy breast milk of the mother condemned to the confinement of her household. I could have given more such examples, but that would be of hardly any use. Is there any home here that has not been cursed by the cries of premature death?

Through these examples it is abundantly clear now that the subjugated life is as harmful for society as the independent life is good for it. Human society is composed of both men and women. The Almighty has created these two sexes and made them mutually dependent on one another in a manner that one without the other can neither grow nor even able to labour. The race that makes for opportunities for these two sexes to work in unison may soon surpass others in advancement. And the race in which one of these two social limbs is alone enabled to labour in an unfettered manner while the other is unable to move forward in any respect finds itself like a lame man left behind. The women like the men have also infinite rights in this world and have a great working space—both must put in equal labour it is true—but the spheres of work need to be so arranged that there should be no possibility of conflict and quarrel among them to disturb peace.

I had hoped that with the progress of social evolution the confinement of Hindu women would be partially slackened, if not altogether removed, and they would find their legitimate scope of work. And with that work their minds would be further cultivated and these cultured Hindu women would once again be worshipped everywhere. But I have already shown that in this country the lives of our women are regressing rather than making gradual progress. That is why I am afraid that in this hour of crisis there must be someone to reverse this direction in very practical terms; we will not be able to manage without such intervention.

Translated by Sourin Bhattacharya

From 'স্বাধীন ও পরাধীন নারীজীবন', প্রদীপ,
ফাল্গুন, ১৩০৪ বঙ্গাব্দ, ফেব্রুয়ারী-মার্চ, ১৮৯৭।

'Swadhin o Paradhin Narijiban', *Pradip*,
Phalgun, 1304 B.S., Feb-March, 1897.

Notes

1 Simanti Sen, ed, *Krishnabhabini Daser Englande Bangamahila* (Calcutta: Stree, 1996).
2 According to Hindu mythology, the earth rests on the multiple heads of Basuki, the serpent king. An earthquake is supposed to occur when Basuki shakes his heads.

7   Anindita Devi

Anindita Devi (1876–1941) was an eminent writer of essays and articles. She wrote a number of sharp feminist pieces under the pseudonym of 'Banganari' (a Bengali woman). Some of her writings were compiled in an anthology, Agamani. *Her essays have been published in* Anindita Devir Rachana Samkalan *(Kolkata: School of Women's Studies, Jadavpur University, 1997). During the period covered by this anthology, Anindita Devi was only a budding writer. It is in the subsequent years that she wrote her major pieces.*

How to Establish Amity among the Different Communities in Bengal

A great man has said, 'National sentiment is but another name for the desire for unity.' Its truth can be verified from examples provided by any progressive civilized race. This sentiment exists so strongly among Europeans that the entire society becomes agitated by the murder of a missionary in a foreign land, and the sun of freedom of that particular country may set forever as penalty for this single offence.

Recently, in this country, the government has had this to say about any political movement, 'These are the opinions of an educated minority to which you belong. This may not be the view of the general public.' No representative can refute this courageously and the movement gets dissipated. The reason for this is lack of unity. Not political movements alone but manufacture and industry come to nothing as a result of this absence of unity. The scientists and historians of our country continually lament the lack of unity.

If there had been cooperation and solidarity among weavers, the ancient art of manufacture of cloth in our country would not have come to such a sorry pass. Enterprises in the recent past, such as the manufacturing of matches in India, would not have died an untimely death otherwise. Even a small task like the manufacture of a pin cannot be successful without mutual cooperation. A country that lacks unity even with sufficient intellectual resources has to wait upon others for everything. It remains indigent even with a fullness of natural riches. Bengal, indeed, the whole of India, is an instance of this. The three qualities of love for one's countrymen, resolution, and patience alone can generate this necessary sentiment of national unity.

Even at the outset, unity cutting across communities seems to be a far cry in relation to Bengal. Where one Hindu does not touch rice cooked by another, never forms marital relations outside the narrowest boundaries of his small schisms, where the inhabitant of one region thinks of someone from a different region as a foreigner due to ignorance of the language, and where people remain fragmented by their separate customs and rituals, the dream of unity among different religious communities seems to be no more than an illusion. Even if we think only of the Hindu community and of the differences with the shudras who are a part of this community we feel appalled. Since the community lives together there is continuous possibility of tension and conflict and yet the root to amity is closed because of discrimination. The hot climatic conditions do not allow anything to solidify. From antiquity India has been known for its absence of unity, with the resulting long foreign domination.

Whatever the adverse conditions may be, today all of us have been brought under the same shadow of British power and we are all known as British subjects. Even if there were no other reasons, this factor might be a powerful bond to unify us. The rise of the Congress also follows from this, but if people in all the provinces do not endeavour to be united in spite of the opportunity and if they do not forget communal feelings then the existence of the Congress can hardly be necessary except for a few days every year. The only outcome of this is to incur the mockery of foreigners.

There is a Provincial Committee here but its only function is the political agitation it conducts for a few days every year. The usefulness of this is not in doubt but varied and consistent efforts are needed to unify all the people of the province.

We are talking about such efforts only in the context of Bengal, but the same things may be applicable to other provinces and if efforts start in one province, others will follow. How can we establish communal amity throughout Bengal! Political objectives may bring us close to one another but the effect of social dissensions is not negligible. This is what must be removed; only then may we be united even while retaining our separate religious beliefs. To realize this objective a great spread of education is absolutely necessary and we have to establish a central organization in Calcutta for the propagation of broadness of mind and fellow-feeling.

Branch organizations should be formed at the village-level. They must arrange for the propagation of Arabic, Persian and Sanskrit and must induct people belonging to one religious faith to the scriptures, literature and sciences of another religious faith. The broadmindedness of great linguists is ample proof of the positive effect of having access to the high cultural texts of people belonging to different religions. Ignorance breeds all superstitions, as education removes ignorance, and a shining picture of the joys, sorrows, aspirations and greatness of other communities is imprinted in our hearts. How then can hatred and suspicion survive there?

If this sense of unity is inculcated among women through education, then each child will imbibe this lesson at its mother's breast. No other form of education can be compared in its depth and permanence with such a lesson. As their ignorance is removed they will be able to refute the prevalent notion that women are opposed to all good things and when they inspire their husbands, sons, fathers, brothers and other relatives to such unity how enthusiastic they will feel. Not only this, they may themselves adopt some of the methods just mentioned to establish amity with women from other communities in Bengal. This shall enhance their broadness of mind and their wisdom. Other good qualities shall blossom apace, their multiplied experience shall add value to whatever suggestions they may make.

Recently, however, most meetings and speeches in this country are organized only for the people concerned to make a name for themselves. The members do not practise what is announced in meetings. The audience takes pleasure in listening to speeches but these speeches do not move them sufficiently to engage in action. Such lethargy spells doom for all meetings and movements which lose credibility in the eyes of ordinary people. They think it impossible that anything worthwhile would emerge from them. The organization mentioned before must achieve credibility through the steadfast endeavour of its members. Whatever you pronounce through speeches you must fulfil in action. If we persevere with our efforts for a long time, maybe one day we shall be successful, and the Bengalis fragmented hundredfold and bereft of power would perhaps be able to enlist their name side by side with those of great and powerful nations. But that success is still a long way off.

Translated by Malini Bhattacharya

From 'বঙ্গদেশের বিভিন্ন সম্প্রদায়ের মধ্যে সদ্ভাব স্থাপনোপায়',
অন্তঃপুর, ১৩০৬ বঙ্গাব্দ, ১৮৯৮।

'Bangadesher Bibhinna Sampradayer Madya Sadbhab Sthapanopay', *Antahpur*, 1306 B.S., 1898.

8 Hemantakumari Chaudhuri

Hemantakumari Chaudhuri (1868–1953) was born in Lahore and sent to Bethune School, Calcutta, when she was twelve years old. Shibnath Sastri, the famous Brahmo scholar, was her guardian. Married at seventeen to Rajchandra Chaudhuri, she accompanied him to Shillong and Sylhet. Deeply committed to women's emancipation, before her marriage, with the encouragement of her father, she had set up a women's society or group at Lahore. A mother to eleven children, she continued to work for women and the underprivileged. While at Shillong she helped to establish a hospital for women. At Sylhet, she organized a meeting where women discussed the plight of the tea gardens' coolies and submitted a petition to the District Commissioner. She went to Patiala as an elderly woman, and at the government's request started the Victoria Memorial School for Girls. She later moved to Dehradun and served as the Municipal Commissioner. She was fluent in Bangla, Hindi and English and a very able speaker. She edited Antahpur *1900–1904 and also wrote many books, among the best known is* Adarsha Mata.

Women's Dress

What are clothes and why do we need them? Clothes are what we wear to cover the body and to preserve modesty. If we read the history of the earth in very early times, we will know that then human beings did not have clothes with which to cover themselves. Members of one tribe might cover their bodies with the bark of trees, another tribe or society or some individual might use animal hide or fur. The proof of this is to be seen even today among many primitive tribes living in dense forests or in mountains. When the Aryans came to India and established their permanent dwelling here, they used to live in dense forests near the Himalayas. They felt the need to cover their bodies primarily because of the cold. Just as the most compassionate Almighty has provided us with many kinds of food for the maintenance of life, so too for bodily protection he has created many kinds of materials from which we can produce coverings for our bodies. Clothes were made from a thread drawn from the bark of trees, as well as from threads spun by silkworms. Thereafter, as man grew more and more civilized, he used his intelligence to make clothes suitable for covering the body from a variety of materials. From books like the *Ramayana* and the *Mahabharata,* we learn how Indian women used a variety of materials for clothing. Forest dwellers covered their bodies with very soft deer skin. The Almighty has made women forever lovers of beauty and modest by nature. In that time, women wore many kinds of clothes such as silk saris of various colours worked in gold, and silver, scarves, mekhalas or long skirts and bodices. It was customary even then to make offerings of clothes to poor widows, brahmins, and married daughters. Of course, geographical difference and the passage of time have brought about a transformation of dress. In the past, in our country, benarasi, nilambari, garad, shantipuri and dhakai saris were held in great esteem. Thereafter, during British rule, the growth of trade and commerce and the improvement of transport facilities resulted in the importing of clothes from many countries.

Gradually the esteem attached to clothes of earlier ages, like benarasi saris, diminished, and their place was taken by Bombay saris or Chinese saris. At present there is no dearth of beautiful and ornate clothes. We have seen how the mode of dress adopted by Indian women has changed in accordance with alterations in social custom and in the country's condition. It will be no exaggeration to say that there is absolutely no resemblance between present-day dress and the style of dress adopted by Aryan women in ancient times. At that time, women had freedom. Aryan women moved freely on the field of battle and in public places like royal assemblies. On many occasions, a wife or a sister might have to accompany her husband or brother on horseback. In consequence, the wearing only of ornate, beautiful clothes was not appropriate for women in those days. There was even some similarity in the style of dressing adopted by women and men. Men wore turbans, and the women of the family drew the end of the sari over their heads, or used a separate scarf or shawl. Women probably pleated their saris in front and drew the other end through their legs to tuck it in behind, to facilitate riding on horses and going into battle. And for this reason, the amount of cloth they used was much greater than the length of our saris. To this day, in the western provinces, Maharashtrian women wear nine or nine-and-a-half yard long saris, in beautiful colours, with borders, pleated at the front and tucked in at the back, and use embroidered bodices and shawls.

In India, the home of many races, one is filled with amazement upon observing the variety of styles in dress. The greatest similarity is that almost everywhere both respectable and common women wear the sari. In the Punjab, women are often seen to wear pyjamas or loose pants. In the northwest and in Rajputana, women wear a flowing skirt, a scarf and a bodice. The Bengali sari is worn everywhere. From the time of the Muslim conquest, the Indian woman, in order to preserve her chastity, has had to remain enclosed in the inner quarters of the house. The kind of thick, long clothes that were needed in ancient times, when the woman had to move about out-of-doors, were now no longer required in a corner of the house away from men's eyes. At that time, women were also deprived of the right to pursue learning and, dressed up like dolls to delight men, were installed in the inner quarters of the house. Following the practice of the begums of those days, Indian women began to use very fine, light weight cloth for their garments. In consequence, the wives of good families in Bengali homes felt no shame in wearing only a single thin sari while going to bathe in the Ganges, or while attending events to which they had been invited and where many people were present. However, at present many have begun to understand that the custom of wearing only a single thin sari is in bad taste, and it is a cause for happiness that this evil habit is gradually disappearing. Thin, fine saris are mostly worn by women of wealthy and respected families. Common women wear thick, coarse saris.

We have always followed others; it might even be said that we have nothing of our own. Given the spread of women's emancipation at the present time, just as there has been change and new development everywhere under its influence, so too there is no doubt that the traditions of Bengali women's dress have undergone improvement. It is impossible to move about freely in front of everyone on all occasions wearing only a single piece of cloth to preserve one's modesty. Even a ten-year-old girl is capable of understanding that one cannot preserve modesty simply by pulling down the end of the sari to veil one's face. Different regions have different tastes. In Maharashtra, neither unmarried nor married women cover their heads. Only widows wear a covering for their heads. Yet in Bengal, both married women and widows cover their heads. In the West, Frenchwomen are celebrated for bringing about changes in dress and heightening its beauty. There is even a special magazine published for the purpose of changing and improving fashions in dress, and women hold meetings and assemblies to introduce new types of clothes. Every day new and attractive fashions, suited to individual seasons, are being launched, and these fashion waves are agitating the society of women in the whole of Europe. One set of every kind of dress, from hats to shoes, worn by our late revered Empress Victoria from infancy to the end of her life, is preserved in her royal palace. To view these items of apparel is to gain special knowledge about the clothes worn by Englishwomen in the nineteenth century.

As a result of the advent of the English race to this country and through intermingling with them, it is not only the case that our husbands, sons and brothers learnt to wear coats and trousers. We too began to use various kinds of chemises, petticoats, bodices and jackets. Prior to this we had no national dress for women, the wearing of which would preserve one's self-respect. Perhaps because of this, many Indian women wore the clothes of the English ladies. Just as there is a difference in strength between English people and Bengalis, so too there is the same difference of strength between the gown and the sari. Many abandon the sari to wear the gown for the sake of convenience in moving about out of doors. At present, women in England are agitating over the issue of whether their traditional dress is injurious to their health, and are taking the opinions of many doctors on this subject. Many have begun to realize the pernicious effects of various diseases arising from the restriction of blood circulation in certain parts of the body. This is caused by the tightlacing of the corsets worn under their clothes from their youth in order to keep their waists slim and their backs straight. It is regrettable that while we have benefited by learning the use of jackets, chemises and other such garments from the English ladies, we are on the other hand harming ourselves and our health is declining by adopting their unhealthy or unsightly apparel because we are enamoured of these opulent, yet unsuitable, clothes. At present a mode of dress has been created for Parsee women, and many have accepted it.[1] Even many women living in domestic seclusion have learnt to wear this dress. I have heard this apparel being praised even by many Englishwomen.

It would be well to discuss whether this dress is generally free from the faults of opulence and foreignness, whether it can be worn by women of all classes according to their means, and whether in the future it can become the common dress of Bengali women. For various reasons, we are becoming poorer day by day. Just as we have to rely on others for food, so too for cloth we are being compelled to look towards Manchester's weavers. Women of Assam and Manipur produce with their own hands the cloth required for the garments of all the members of their families. Many poor women earn their livelihoods by weaving cloth and selling it. No other race in India is as dependent on others as Bengalis. The Bengali woman is draped from head to foot in foreign clothes. Although dhakai, benarasi, and shantipuri dhotis and saris are sometimes used, they are expensive. Nowadays, since beautiful British-made saris of various colours are cheaply available, no one is much inclined to buy indigenous saris at a high price. Therefore when considering the use of clothes, we should think of all aspects of the matter. On the one hand, just as lower costs are desirable, so too is it essential to wear a neat dress suitable for protecting health and modesty. The chief fault of women is that when ten or twenty of them assemble, they begin to discuss the cost and beauty of dresses. And in such assemblies, poor women suffer shame and insult. In actual fact, excess in price is not always an index of the beauty or decency of dress. Rather, in particular cases, it may be seen that even after wearing an expensive dress, one is unable to produce an impression of its cost or beauty owing to the lack of a sense of neatness and propriety; whereas another person, wearing a dress which costs very little, can make it eye-catching.

Translated by Supriya Chaudhuri

From 'মহিলার পরিচ্ছদ', অন্তঃপুর, আষাঢ়, ১০০৮ বঙ্গাব্দ, জুন-জুলাই, ১৯০১।

'Mahilar Paricchad', *Antahpur*, Asharh, 1308 B.S., June-July, 1901.

Note

1 The Parsee way of wearing the sari over a petticoat and with a long-sleeved blouse was adapted by Jnanadanandini Devi, who made it fashionable for Bengali women, and it gained widespread acceptance all over India as the dress for the modern Indian woman. See also 15, Swarnakumari Devi, 'Words from Times Past' and 16, Sarala Devi Chaudhurani, 'My Life Changes Track', this volume.

9   Kumudini Mitra

Kumudini Mitra (1882–1943), the daughter of a leading Brahmo, Krishnakumar Mitra, and of Lilavati, the daughter of Rajnarayan Bose, a famous Brahmo scholar and nationalist, was an early graduate of the University of Calcutta. She married Sachindraprasad Bose. She was deeply involved in nationalist politics, especially the opposition to the Partition of Bengal (1905) and the ensuing Swadeshi movement. She wrote many patriotic books, Sikher Balidan, *a biography,* Jehangirer Atmajibani, *and a life of Mary Carpenter, the English social reformer. She edited* Suprabhat *(1907–1914) and* Bangalakshmi *(1925–1927).*

What Women Should Do When the Motherland Is in Distress

The mutual interests of the conquerors and the conquered always contradict each other. If the conquered, however, are very much inferior to the conquerors in culture and in power, and if the conquerors have nothing at stake, then the latter sometimes are not averse to giving some benefits to the former. Such instances are not lacking in history. When the British colonized this country, proud of their power they saw no reason to take seriously the powerless Indians who were ignorant in modern sciences, unacquainted with the progressive thoughts of civilized nations and riven with internal dissensions. Hence out of pity, while keeping their own interests intact, they sought to do good to the country to the extent possible.

However, under more favourable circumstances, as a result of their contact with the civilized British, the fragmented nationalities of India are now about to develop into a great nation; national sentiments, a sense of national unity, are beginning to inspire this degraded people. These signs of a national awakening are stirring up a great anxiety in the hearts of our rulers, as being inimical to the British interest. This has reached a climax during the reign of the present Governor General [Viceroy], Lord Curzon.[1] When we look at the various measures taken by Lord Curzon, it seems to us that these conceal an effort to stem the flow of development of the people of this country. Self-improvement is hampered if a person is continually reminded of his insignificance and weakness. Curzon seems to be telling Indians at every step, you are subjects and therefore to be pitied, we are the ruling race, you must accept with bowed heads whatever deals we implement for you. He tries to tell us that he knows what is good for us better than we do, but Indians are not enamoured of such political selflessness. The Calcutta Municipal Act,[2] the University Act,[3] the act regarding official secrets, the restrictions on access for Indians into the administrative sphere and the curtailment of power of the native princes, and so on, are not regarded by Indians as anything but the severe whiplash of those in power. The intention is the same everywhere.

The Bengalis are today most advanced so far as political movements are concerned. The regional languages are acquiring parity in status, the opening of railways and waterways, the central position of the capital, centralized administration, English education, and so on, are raising the Bengalis to the position of a powerful nation. Lord Curzon has dealt a hammer blow at the roots of this national unity by dividing Bengal. One stroke from his pen has opened up the road to downfall for an advanced and powerful nation. All the appeals, arguments, movements of the entire Bengali nation have become futile against the hard attitude of the bureaucrats. The dark clouds that had been gathering on the Indian horizon for a few years have today covered the whole sky. The sharp hatred and contempt of foreign rulers for a nation that had been trying to raise its head and stand on its own feet has brought all its efforts to nought. Everybody in this country now knows how degraded a colonized nation is. As an arrogant elephant tramples an unarmed and helpless person with impunity so are our rulers crushing our national good under their feet, deaf to all arguments and appeals.

But have all our efforts been defeated? No, never; now it is entirely up to us to keep Bengal whole and to work towards our own improvement. The British depend completely on trade. Goods produced in Britain worth millions of rupees are sold in Bengal. If Bengalis resolve to boycott British goods, in case they are impervious to our appeals, then we shall be able to disrupt their trade. This would disturb the entire British nation. British traders are so powerful that their parliament is but an instrument in their hands. Parliament cannot ignore the interests of British traders; hence 20,000 Bengalis gathering in the Calcutta Town Hall have resolved to boycott British goods so long as the government refuses to listen to them. This has created a great enthusiasm and excitement in the country. Are not our women touched by the heat of this patriotic fire? Should not women observe the same vows that the patriots have taken in the name of their country? In these dark days what hope is there if women do not join in this boycott with their men?

The love for foreign fashions and foreign goods has entered into our veins and bones. Our neglect of indigenous goods has destroyed indigenous manufacturing capacity. We are forced to depend on a foreign country even for small things. If we had not been so enamoured of showy foreign goods, harmful for our country, then today there might have been sufficient production of indigenous goods. Our weavers go hungry today because we rejected the cloth made by them. We have facilitated the prosperity of foreigners while harming our own interests. Does not this misfortune of our country affect our women? Are they not going to find means to prevent this? When the nation is in danger will women fail to be inspired by patriotism? Think of this hallowed land where at one time virtuous and heroic women used to cut off their long hair to provide bowstrings to save the country, where they used to willingly send their husbands and sons to war, and where they themselves went to the battlefield to fight. Will the women of that land remain weak, lifeless and uninspired? Will they not even take the simple vow of not using foreign clothes for the good of their country? Have centuries of servitude made us so forgetful about our duties to the hallowed land of our birth? Do not our hearts throb for our poverty-stricken country? No good son or daughter of the motherland can conceivably behave in this way.

Let us find out what the women of Japan would do in a national crisis. What patriotism, what self-sacrifice are they not showing right in front of our eyes! From the empress down to the beggar woman, all of them are eager to serve their country.[4] The aristocratic lady, unused to carrying even a small burden, is nursing the ordinary soldier without the slightest hesitation. The mother is sacrificing her life lest she stands in the way of her son's service to the country. Can we not follow their example even slightly in this matter? Why should we lie in a death-like state when by birth we belong to the country inhabited earlier by Aryan women of unforgettable prowess? Why should women lag behind men in patriotic sentiments? Men will never succeed in this auspicious work unless women unite with them resolutely to seek the country's welfare. Let us take the vow: 'If indigenous goods are available, we shall not buy foreign goods and whatever is not indigenously produced we shall buy from other countries except Britain.'

It is easy to take a vow but difficult to keep it. Let us not break our resolution tempted by foreign luxuries. The time for buying for the Puja [Durga Puja] has come, let the women of Bengal, resolute in their unity, vow in the name of the motherland that they are not going to buy foreign clothes this year. Is it not more honourable to use ordinary clothes produced in our own country than to wear expensive foreign clothes? Does it not fill our hearts with pleasure when we think 'these are of my own country?' In Japan clothes are woven by close relatives, by mothers, sisters, friends, they never have to rely on others for their clothes—this is a matter of great pride for Japanese women. When America faced such a crisis the Americans resolved not to buy British goods and rich American women did not mind wearing inferior garments produced in their own country. Indeed, this added to their honour.

Today in our country attractive fabrics, scissors, knives, and so on, are being produced. Let us decide that we shall altogether refrain from using a number of foreign articles like clothes, salt, sugar and matches. The boycott of at least these goods will go a long way. Not only must we keep this promise but also actively try to persuade relatives, neighbours and all the women living in the village to take this vow. Hindu women still endure many hardships while observing vows taken for the welfare of fathers, brothers, husbands and sons. Shall we be tardy in observing these simple restrictions for our motherland, higher even than heaven for us? Is not the Indian woman more used to taking vows and maintaining them? If piles of British clothes worth crores of rupees remain unsold in the season of the Puja, the impact of this will be felt in England and the government will be forced to withdraw the order for partitioning Bengal. So, let the men and women in each family get together and implement their vow and thus make their lives meaningful. Let foreigners be impressed by the patriotism, resoluteness and enthusiasm of docile and weak Bengalis. Let us not give them the opportunity to mock at us as Bengalis who are good only with words. In this time of crisis can we not be united to keep our resolve? Shall we remain unconcerned about the distress of our motherland and lick the feet of our foreign masters? Let us wake up, forcefully repel all difficulties, and advance to the field of work.

Translated by Malini Bhattacharya

From 'মাতৃভূমির দুর্দিনে মহিলাদিগের কর্তব্য' ভারত-মহিলা,
ভাদ্র, ১৩১২ বঙ্গাব্দ, আগস্ট-সেপ্টেম্বর, ১৯০৫।

'Matribhumir Durdine Mahiladiger Kartabya', *Bharat-Mahila*, Bhadra, 1312 B.S., Aug-Sept, 1905.

Notes

1   A British aristocrat who rose fast in the British Conservative Party, and became the under secretary of state for India, Lord Curzon became

the Viceroy of India, 1898–1905. A vigorous administrator who instituted many measures for the benefit of India, eg, the Archaeological Department that was later to unearth the Indus Valley civilization, the Panjab Land Alienation Act that protected cultivators from eviction for debt, and railway expansion, adding 6000 miles of track, he was thoroughly hostile to political reform and nationalist aspirations, of which the Partition of Bengal, 1905, is a prime example. See also 13, Khairunnisa Khatun, 'Patriotism', n2.

2   Act of 1899 that reduced the number of Indian members to the Calcutta Corporation.

3   Act of 1904 that added postgraduate studies and a residential system but increased the number of nominated members to governing bodies at the expense of the teaching staff of the affiliated colleges, members of the new middle class, who would be displaced. As the only Indian member of the Universities Commission, 1902, whose recommendations were embodied in the Act, Sir Gurudas Banerjee disagreed strongly with it.

4   The Russo-Japanese war, 1905, when Japan defeated Russia and provided an example of a victory by an Asian country over a European one.

10   Kamini Roy

Kamini Roy (1864–1933) was born into a Brahmo family that favoured social reform and education for women (her sister Jamini qualified as a doctor), she became one of the first women graduates of India (B. A. Sanskrit Hons) from Bethune College, where she later taught. Precocious, her book of poems Alo o Chhaya *was published when she was fifteen. She came from a world that was exposed to westernization; her father, Chandicharan Sen, was a subjudge who also had literary interests, and her husband, Kedarnath Roy, was a civil servant. She published many books of poetry,* Mahasweta o Pundarik, Malya o Nirmalya, *to mention a few. She was co-chairperson of the Bangiya Sahitya Parishad (1932–1933). She was one of the investigators of the Women Labourers Commission (1922–1923). She was presented with the Jagattarini Gold Medal by the University of Calcutta in recognition of her contribution to literature and scholarship.*

The Fruit of the Tree of Knowledge

The English poet Gray has observed: 'Where ignorance is bliss, 'tis folly to be wise.'[1]

The story of the first man and woman in the Old Testament of the Bible also speaks thus. According to the Bible, mankind's thirst for knowledge is the original sin and the source of all human sorrow and misery. Partaking of the fruit of the Tree of Knowledge has subjected humans to disease and illness, old age and death, violence and grief or else they could have enjoyed eternal youth, immortality, and a blessed life beyond pain and suffering in heavenly Eden.

One wonders why knowledge—which lends eyes to the blind, bestows strength unto the weak, destroys distances, and brings infinite powers within human grasp—is regarded as evil and the constant companion of darkness in ancient Jewish religious texts whereas in reality it is more like the holy, bright, life-giving light. Yet there is a profound truth embedded in this ancient narrative. A whole world of human woes would have vanished if we did not have a sense of good and evil. Animals cannot distinguish between honesty and dishonesty, well-being and illness, truth and lies, virtue and vice. Hence they are untroubled by any feeling of shame, internal remorse or external punishment. Where there is no knowledge, there is neither depravity nor piety.

But why should knowledge—which has invested mankind with true humanity and elevated him from the status of beasts, has made him the descendant of the Gods and which is indeed a rare gift from the Almighty—bring such sufferings to the human race and how?

When the first man, Adam, and the first woman, Eve, standing on the brink of knowledge, exchanged glances, their comely faces must have reflected the bashful rosy hue of a blooming flower. I do not know whether they considered the new gamut of emotions, never experienced before, sad or happy. Is it likely that it was shot through with searing agony? Did they not feel on that fateful day that although they were bound by the closest ties and were each inseparable from the other, they inhabited two different bodies: that the whole universe was a strange entity outside their single unified existence? Did not the combined worship of beauty and restraint start on the day when they first covered their nakedness with leaves?

A new current of thoughts and actions to sustain and please each other displaced the indolent stasis of their hitherto placid and idle lives. Did this not enrich and beautify their hearts even more? Had not the evening rest after their daily labour been sweetened by the knowledge of togetherness and mutual companionship? Had not compassion, generated by approaching dangers and tribulations, intensified their conjugal love? See how sweat-stained Adam relaxes under the sweet words and gentle care of his wife, the exertion of tilling the land is completely forgotten. And again observe how Eve, who has just become a mother, discounts all physical pain as she clutches her newborn baby to her breast.

It is useless to debate whether it is a curse or a blessing for a man to toil for his wife and child, for a woman to spend her life looking after her husband and son. To live solely for oneself is pointless. Dying for another makes even death seem desirable. A sense of *'for the sake of another'* is very important in life.

Human beings were no better than animals in their infancy; with the aid of knowledge, they gradually developed and approached divinity. In the Bible God says, 'See how man has become like us—he can discriminate between the good and the bad.' The Lord has banished him from the Garden of Eden lest he reaches out for the fruit of the Tree of Life and becomes immortal. The Tree of Knowledge and the Tree of Life were beside each other, and still are. Yet even now, after millions of years, people still refer to knowledge as the *Poison Tree*. The biblical God was against human access to knowledge; in the new society, one class has always sowed thorns in the path of another class trying to gain knowledge, and continues to do so. The sole reason for this is the age-old fear of losing one's primacy—'lest they become like us'. The priestly community has for long attempted to monopolize the scriptures—the repository of knowledge. Their overpowering domination derived from their knowledge of the ancient texts. In order to perpetuate their dominance over the lower orders and the women, they took every care to keep them away from the light of learning.

The male desire to rule is the primary if not the only stumbling block to women's enlightenment. We often notice that lack of practice renders education futile. Because women are also mothers they have much less leisure than men to nurture their acquired knowledge. Just as the dual role of the wife and the mother has circumscribed the women's zone of functioning, it has also constricted their period of study. Are women unhappy because of this? It is not possible to answer this question with a single word at this juncture. A large number of women, and men too, are indifferent, even averse to the idea of learning. Yet the kind of educational facilities available for men are not available for women. Not all men pursue knowledge after entering family life; most are busy with their business or profession. But the road to education for women is barred from before because they *will* be embroiled in domesticity and household work. One who is born blind does not pine for light. But one who has had a glimpse and then shut out of its radiance is infinitely more wretched. Such unhappy and deprived women are not rare upon this earth.

The entire human race is progressing inexorably with the light of knowledge. Wisdom acquired through tremendous hardships many centuries ago by the learned elders of the community is now readily available to people as inherited wealth from their childhood. New knowledge is opening fresh avenues of pain, joy, desire and aspiration, awakening novel forces and energies. Despite living in this enlightened world and acknowledging the need to educate and instruct men of the lower classes, the people of this country are totally apathetic towards women's literacy. They are extremely afraid and suspicious of women's emancipation. Why? The same old fear—'Lest they become like us.' But is this at all possible? Woman, will the light of knowledge dazzle you to such an extent that you will ignore the sweet virtues of motherhood and sisterhood, and eagerly adopt the authoritarian ways of your father! Can that be true learning, which does not teach you to discriminate between the beneficial and the harmful, the beautiful and the ugly, the useful and the useless? Cradled in your mother's arms, you have been nurtured by the white nectar flowing from her breasts and in time you yourself will become a 'mother'—*the abiding deity of affection/the embodiment of love*—I fail to understand how you can fall from womanhood. Can you?

Even if one concedes that in certain spheres women may 'become like us' how does that harm 'us'? In the *Puranas* we see that when a man or a demon engaged in austere, steadfast meditation, Indra and the other Gods, afraid that he might wrest their divinity, tried to disrupt his prayers. Are 'we' assailed by similar fears?

Men highlight certain faults in order to prove that women are deficient. Will it help or hinder society if women are freed of these shortcomings through enlightenment and education, if courage and tranquility replace timidity and ignorance, if fickle minds become resolute, if women escape charges of shortsightedness by weighing the pros and cons before acting, if they discard bias and dispense rewards with a steady hand upholding the scales of justice? Will home and family be greatly imperilled if women act with responsibility instead of being mere mechanical dolls, can comprehend the meaning of the prayers they chant instead of merely parroting them, can sweep away superstition and appreciate the real significance, poetry, beauty and utility of hereditary practices and rituals?

The sorrows entailed in acquiring wisdom have been stated earlier. If one can identify good as good then that which is evil is bound to disquiet the mind. With knowledge, new aspirations are born; new goals beckon; virtue resides in following one's ideal; the opposite is vice. Every article of knowledge imposes a responsibility over our moral lives. In this sense enlightenment is indeed the source of grief. But the difference between animals and human beings, learning and ignorance, is this distinctive suffering.

On the other hand there is a permanent connection between knowledge and happiness. Wherever there is wisdom there is light. Error, doubt and fear cannot survive there. It is a world of pure, joyous, meaningful existence; had it been otherwise human life would have been nothing but a burden.

Translated by Sarbani Choudhury

From 'জ্ঞানবৃক্ষের ফল', ভারত মহিলা, আশ্বিন, ১৩১২ বঙ্গাব্দ, সেপ্টেম্বর-অক্টোবর, ১৯০৫।

'Gyanbriksher Phal', *Bharat Mahila*, Aswin, 1312 B.S, Sept-Oct, 1905.

Note

1 Thomas Gray (1716–91), 'Ode on a Distant Prospect on Eton College', 1747.

11 Begum Rokeya Sakhawat Hossain

Begum Rokeya Sakhawat Hossain (1880–1932), a brilliant writer and social reformer far ahead of her time, was taught at home, learning English from her older brother. At eighteen, she married Sakhawat Hossain of Bhagalpur, who supported the education of women. Ten years later, after his death, she came to Calcutta and immersed herself in social reform, undertaking pioneering work within the Muslim community. In 1911 she founded the Sakhawat Memorial School in Calcutta with eight pupils. In 1916 she founded the Anjuman-Khawateen-i-Islam to work for the welfare and uplift of Muslim women. A fighter for social justice and social reform, her writings are relevant even today. This is especially so for 'Abarodhbasini' (Those dwelling in seclusion) and Sultana's Dream, *which she wrote in English, a fantasy where women rule and men are secluded.* Motichur, *vols 1 and 2, comprise her prose writings. She also wrote a novel,* Padmarag.

The Worship of Women

I

'The honour that Hindus accord women is certainly laudable,' I said, leafing through an old issue of the periodical *Bharati*.[1] In no other country is such respect shown towards woman. Woman is the Hindus' deity of worship.'

At my words the women present burst out laughing. I was slightly disconcerted. Jamila Begum said, protesting, 'Forgive me, Mrs. Chatterjee! In this country, the role of a woman is not superior to that of a maidservant.'

Jamila is the wife of a famous lawyer; she is a great friend of Kusumkumari Ray. The other lady present, Amena Begum, is a widow; she lived in western India for ten years, and knows Urdu very well. She is also a dear friend of Kusum. They are so intimate with Mrs. Ray that they address each other by their first names. It has been only two or three months since I became acquainted with these Muslim women, but Kusum is the same age as I am, and a childhood friend of mine.

It was in Kusum's sitting-room that I was sitting and leafing through *Bharati*. I had not been prepared for an argument—nevertheless, quite a debate ensued upon my remark. Amena Begum smiled a little and said, 'In this country women are a kind of personal property belonging to men.'

I: This is a mistake on your part. If Hindus did not respect women, they would not have viewed them as Goddesses. Most of their deities are women.

Amena: But we would wish to judge after seeing the practical results. Leave aside the myth making, and show us true events.

I: Kusum! Help me. Bring your *Mahabharata*. We shall show them historical events.

Kusum: I respect all of you equally, so I can't favour any one. What is the good of the *Mahabharata* or history? You should discuss contemporary social events.

I (to the two Muslim ladies): Do you want to call Damayanti, Sita, Savitri, and other daughters of India mere serving maids?

Jamila: No, Sita and Savitri became famous because of their own good qualities. Sita was a virtuous person, but how did society 'worship' her during her lifetime?

I	(not answering them): In ancient times there were many Goddesses. Such learned women as Lilavati and Khana are unique in the world.[2]
Amena:	They were learned, and that virtue was their very own. But the discussion here is about the treatment of women by society. Khana was exceptionally proficient in astronomy. Even now, there isn't a farmer in the countryside who doesn't know a few of Khana's precepts. But—
I:	But what? The fact that Khana's precepts are recited from village to village shows that Khana is worshipped by the mass of the people.
Amena:	Forgive me, Mrs. Chatterjee. Let me finish what I was saying. Khana may be worshipped now, but don't you know how she died? She was killed by having her tongue cut out, the tongue that gave birth to those precepts.
I:	She was not killed. But, yes, her tongue was cut out.
Jamila:	Why shouldn't we call that killing? After her husband cut her tongue out, Khana gazed at her husband silently, wept, and died.
Kusum:	Leave aside these old matters. Let victory and defeat be decided by events of this century.
I:	I am alone, while the Begum Sahibas are two. Victory belongs to the strong, so I shall accept defeat without war.
Kusum:	What? Why should you abandon the argument so soon? Advance as far as you can.
Amena:	Even if there are two of us, on the whole we are weaker than you are since you have received higher education (even if you have failed the F.A.!)[3] You have gathered experience by seeing and hearing many things and by reading various books. And we live under strict purdah— we know only Kusum and you.
I:	Well, all right, since you won't let me be! Kusum! Is not the present century fourteenth by the Bengali calendar?

	Wouldn't that mean the twentieth century of the Christian era?
Kusum:	Be it the fourteenth or the twentieth century. Why don't you consider events that have occurred in the last hundred years?
I:	Very well. Recently, with the creation of the Brahmo Samaj, women have reached the status of real Goddesses, this takes them beyond their earlier merely imagined deification.
Jamila:	That is partly true. But take something else on board too—since you take pride in the Goddesses of Hindu society, you should also be prepared to take on board the faults of that society.
I:	That is a very hard condition.
Kusum:	It is just, even if it is hard, They have sealed off your escape from beforehand—do you get it, Prabha?
I:	What sort of escape?
Kusum:	Had they talked about the plight of some helpless woman belonging to a Hindu family, you might have said, 'But that sort of thing doesn't happen in our Brahmo Samaj.'
I:	That is true. Can anyone say that helpless women are oppressed in the Brahmo Samaj?
Amena:	If you go only by the Nababidhan sect of the Brahmo Samaj, then why drag in Hindu Goddesses? It is really unjust for you to come forward and accept praise for the virtues, and yet refuse to accept blame for the vices.
Jamila:	Now I have understood why you were accepting defeat without war. Well, then, let's not discuss the worship of women, let's talk about something else.
I:	At first, I was unsure as to what I should do next; a little while later I thought, 'Am I such a coward that I shall concede defeat without argument?' Outwardly, I said, 'No Begum Sahiba! Fear not—I shall not turn my back—let us go on!'

Everyone burst into laughter. To make them laugh had been precisely my intention. But for reasons of etiquette, they were no longer discussing social issues. I found this intolerable, so I remained adamant and said: 'Well, Begum Sahiba, you have not been able to tell the story of a single oppressed woman.'

Jamila: Why only one, one could tell many—who will count the hundreds of flames in that fire?

I: Show me at least one such flame!

Jamila: Very well. We can hear it in the voice of the Hindu women who are worshipped:

'Bravo, children of Hindus!
Are your hearts made of stone?
. . . .
You mangle the scriptures to kill girls.
. . . .
They have no compassion and no religion,
They cannot distinguish between deeds and misdeeds,
They chew up girls, citing the scriptures.'

What do you say to this? Shall I call those words a scream of anguish from a wounded heart, or a benediction given in pleasure at being worshipped?

I: That is a poet's composition—imagined anguish.
Jamila: You call the anguish of a child widow imagined pain?
Amena: It is not entirely imagined, rather, it is largely true.
Kusum: Absolutely true.
Amena: But it is the social custom, so one can be forced to put up with it. Leaving aside questions of poetic imagination, I shall show you right now with what ingredients India worships women—for examples of that we shall not have to go far. Have you seen the book *Heart-Beats* by Pratapchandra Mozoomdar?[4]

My first thought was that the book discusses only spiritual things. I thought a little and then said bravely, 'Yes, I have seen it. It does not propound any theory about the oppression of women.'

II

Amena: Although it is not found in the book itself, one gets an example in Mr. S. G. Barrow's biography of Mr. Mozoomdar.[5]

I: An example of the oppression of a helpless woman? In the brief biography of the teacher?

Amena said in a steady voice: 'Yes, the incident of his mother's death. When Mr. Mozoomdar's mother, suffering from cholera, was in her death throes, the head of the household was sleeping peacefully. If the cow belonging to the household had been ill, perhaps the master of the house would not have remained unworried. The treatment of widows by society comes through wonderfully in Mr. Mozoomdar's words: re-read pages fourteen to sixteen in the biography. It breaks one's heart to read them. Even pet dogs and cats don't perhaps die without medical care; and yet the best among God's creations, the wife in a family, is restless in the pangs of sickness—and no one takes a second look at her! No one thought that a doctor should be called for the widow. Mozoomdar himself was about to go and interrupt the contented sleep of his uncle, but he was unable to enter the room inhabited by the master of the household. Even the servant would not go and call a doctor—even if he wouldn't, the son could not remain tranquil. Can anyone whose mother is saying farewell forever remain inert? No. He ran out into the street like a madman. He tried to call [the late] Keshabchandra Sen and some other friends. But everyone's door was closed at night. He went to the house of a certain doctor—but the doctor's servant turned the poor man out! The servant was after all an Indian man: he certainly knew how to worship women. So he thought that it was not right disturb his master for the sake of a widow, and he turned away a son grieving for his mother.

In our mind's eye we can clearly see that nineteen-year-old boy running about in the streets, nearly maddened with grief because of his mother. And we can feel the yearning and the terrible anguish in his heart. Among the various blessings of God that we enjoy, a mother is the greatest blessing. Let happiness and prosperity be put on one side of a pair of scales, and the mother on the other side.

If you call this, the heartless, ruthless treatment of widows, the 'worship of women', then I have nothing more to say.

I: Such incidents are rare, not everyone can be deemed guilty because one widow has not been treated with care.

Kusum: No, Prabha! Such incidents are not rare—rather, it is the case that no one else records such scandalous stories as Mr. Mozoomdar did, so we don't get to know of such incidents.

I (to Jamila Begum): And you? Do you know of any hair-raising incident?

Jamila: I have seen an incident with my own eyes—it is a long story.

I: Tell us, we shall listen.

Jamila said, 'The little daughter of a rich man was ill. In their house, they had servants, a coach and horses, and every possible item of luxury. However, the little girl was not receiving medical treatment because girls were considered a curse.

There was no dearth of anything—the other children would toss around money in their play, yet this child, yet to be weaned, was dying without medical care. The mistress of the house could not bear this. With tears in her eyes, she entreated the head of the household to call a doctor, but he did not heed her. One day when the master was going to the doctor for his own sake, the mistress said, 'Do tell the doctor about our little girl's condition.' 'Do girls ever die?' said the master, and left.

Then the helpless lady, having no other recourse, took the ailing child in her lap and continued to weep silently. When the father langur tries to kill the baby male langur, the langur mother clasps the child to her bosom and saves its life by fleeing to the jungle. But where can a woman in purdah go to save her baby girl from a father's oppression? There are innumerable doctors in the city—nevertheless, how does that benefit the dweller of the 'inner apartments'?

I: Can man be so heartless? What happened in the end? Did the baby survive, or did she die of neglect?

Jamila: In the end the baby survived. When the mother was crying with her daughter in her lap, providentially the fortunate eldest son of that family had entered the inner apartments. He was not yet an adult, so his tender heart grieved, and he himself went to the doctor and brought some doses of medicine. He had brought the medicine only to console his mother! By the grace of God, the little girl survived by dint of that small amount of medicine. That rich family still lives there. That child, that father, mother, brother—all are living!

I: Is this family Hindu or Muslim?

Jamila: I shall not divulge that. What is the good of smearing ink on their faces? It is enough to say that they are Bengalis.

I: Look, the heinous custom of total purdah prevalent in this country is the root of all ills. Muslim society is steeped in this. Muslim women are utterly helpless because they don't even appear before servants. Purdah has made them inferior to and more helpless than animals such as the langur mothers.

III

Amena: Though the custom of total purdah is disgusting, it has become part of our flesh and bone. Until men learn to be decent and courteous, it won't be easy to leave purdah. If men had learnt to show due respect to women, then there would be no problem!

Kusum: I have heard that in other countries where Muslims are in the majority such a custom of purdah is absent. Then why did Muslims in India create this sort of purdah and make us captive along with their own wives and daughters?

Jamila: Who is the creator of purdah? No one has been able to determine that. When a Muslim brother writes in favour of purdah, he says, 'It is we who are the creators of purdah; the claim that our Hindu brothers make that they invented purdah is not correct.' And then again, the Hindu brother who writes in favour of purdah adduces arguments to say, 'Muslims have learnt the custom of purdah from non-Muslims.' In any case, whoever the creator of purdah may be, it is we who are suffering its consequences.

I: Why don't you gradually abandon purdah? We have done it.

Jamila: Your abandoning of purdah has hardly been lauded. You have had to hear a lot of vilification because of the way in which you have left purdah.

I: Why fear such villification?

Amena: You may not fear it, but many have stepped beyond the limits of natural modesty, and in some cases the loss of purity—

I: Why did you stop? Go on.

Amena: I was about to say something unpleasant; anyway we have certain duties towards society as well, which we cannot neglect simply for our personal comfort.

I: Hindus villify the Brahmo Samaj baselessly, and I see no need for heeding them.

Kusum: But one should be careful after listening to the negative things that the Brahmo Samaj itself says about leaving

	purdah. Perhaps Amena was about to report something which she had heard about the Brahmo Samaj.
Amena:	You infer correctly.
I:	But, on the whole, the degree of oppression of women that takes place in Muslim societies does not happen anywhere else. You spoke of Khana's death, but do you know the history of the Anarkali mausoleum in Lahore? Anarkali was buried alive on Akbar's orders.[6] Afterwards Emperor Jehangir had the beautiful mausoleum built over Anarkali's corpse. Who knows whether some sad story lies hidden inside the Taj Mahal as well?
Jamila:	It is true that the Muslims oppress women, but they don't practise deception in public by saying 'we worship women'. Rather the wooden, orthodox mullahs of our country think that it is their religious duty to oppress women.
Amena:	I think that Hindus have learnt the custom of purdah from us, and that the hardened mullahs have learnt to treat women more cruelly from the Hindus. Otherwise, if one goes by the prescriptions of the Koran Sharif, neither the oppression of women nor the custom of purdah is acceptable.
I:	Do you believe that orthodox mullahs are in favour of an unjust system of purdah?
Jamila:	Look, Amena, don't you go throwing stones at the beehive of the mullahs now.
Amena:	Yes, you are right. Now I am not prepared to throw stones at the mullahs' beehive. Let's stop talking about mullahs, Mrs. Chatterjee.
I:	If you are afraid of bees, how will you gather honey?
Jamila:	Before gathering honey, one takes care to light a fire and raise smoke in advance, and then one can bear the stings of one or two bees. But it would be childish foolishness to throw stones at the hive without making preparations for gathering honey. Here we are talking about the oppression of women, speak of that.
I:	That is something that you will speak about, and I'll listen to.

Amena: There was of course so much to say—there is no end of such heart-rending stories. But today there is no more time. We will go now, Kusum.
So we returned to our respective homes.

Translated by Barnita Bagchi

From 'নারী-পূজা', মহিলা, পৌষ-মাঘ, ফাল্গুন, ১৩১২ বঙ্গাব্দ, ডিসেম্বর, ১৯০৫-মার্চ, ১৯০৬।

'Nari-Puja', *Mahila, Pous*, Magh, Phalgun, 1312 B.S., Dec, 1905-March, 1906.

Notes

1 A literary magazine published from the Tagore household that had widespread influence on the literary world of Bengal (1877–1926). It was edited initially by Dwijendranath Tagore and subsequently by Rabindranath Tagore, Swarnakumari Devi, Sarala Devi Chaudhurani and Hiranmoyee Devi. See also 15, Swarnakumari Devi, 'Words from the Past' and 16, Sarala Devi Chaudhurani, 'My Life Chagnes Track', this volume.

2 Lilavati, see 2, Kailashbasini Devi, 'The Woeful Plight of Hindu Women', n12.

    Khana was the wife of Mihir and the daughter-in-law of Varaha, two eminent astrologers in the court of Vikramaditya (A.D. fourth century), though some accounts state that Varahamihir was one person and one of the 'nine jewels' of the royal court. Khana, according to legend, surpassed both her husband and her father-in-law in astrological calculations, as a result of which she too was invited to join the court. Fearing that Khana's fame would eclipse theirs, Mihir is said to have cut out Khana's tongue upon the order of his father, which caused her death. In Bengali proverbs Khana is mentioned in connection with agricultural and season-al lore.

3 First Arts or the examination held at the end of the first year of college.

4 P. C. Mozoomdar, *Heart-Beats*. Biographical sketch by Samuel J. Barrows (Calcutta: Nababidhan Publising Committee, 1935).

5 Pratapchandra Mozoomdar (1840–1905), joined the Brahmo Samaj in 1859, and after the Brahmo Samaj split, he remained with

Keshabchandra's Nababidhan group. He travelled to many countries as a preacher and also attended the world conference on religion held in Chicago in 1893. He edited a number of newspapers and journals and was associated with the Calcutta University Institute, and was one of the biographers of Keshabchandra. See also n4.

6 A court singer and dancer in the Mughal court and Prince Selim, the son and heir of Emperor Akbar, fell in love. In order to put an end to this relationship Akbar supposedly had Anarkali sealed up alive in a tomb. Whether true or not, a tomb exists in Lahore. This love story has stirred the imagination of folk poets through the ages.

12   Hiranmoyee Devi

Hiranmoyee Devi (1870–1925) was the eldest daughter of Swarnakumari Devi and Janakinath Ghosal and granddaughter of Maharshi Debendranath Tagore. She started writing poetry as a child; her first published poem possibly appeared in Sakha *in December 1883. Aged fifteen, she was married to Phanibhushan Mukherjee, professor of chemistry and biology. Her husband's work took them to many parts of the country including Rajshahi and Indore. She gave birth to several children, most of whom died in infancy. Her prose and poetry were mainly published in* Bharati o Balak. *For some time she edited* Bharati *herself, later co-editing it with her younger sister Sarala Devi. When Swarnakumari Devi started Sakhi Samiti for educating women, Hiranmoyee became its head and was responsible for running it. She started a women's handicrafts association for poor widows at her residence. She will be remembered for many such philanthropic initiatives. Her writings have not been translated before.*

Proposal: A Women's Arts Association

There are two objectives of setting up such an association: one is obvious from its name, to train up women in arts and crafts. The other is to inculcate a love for our country among women. That such training would benefit women immensely is beyond doubt, given the fact that the rich, the poor and the middle class all value beauty. It is true that affluent households want for nothing, but the joy associated with using things handcrafted by women of the family cannot compare with handicrafts bought from the market. Besides, enjoying art for art's sake is only possible in affluent households. For the middle class, the more the women learn to make things of utility at home, the better. Our expenses have gone up because of various reasons these days, buying readymade garments being one. If housewives learnt to tailor these, they would save expenses. As joint families break up, quite a few widows of respectable families find it difficult to cope. It is essential to arrange some kind of training for them. Women usually invest in gold the moment they are able to save some money in the hope that it will come in handy at times of distress. Their training in arts and crafts should stand them in better stead. When an ornament is sold off, the money that comes in is spent in no time, whereas their training would be a lifelong asset. In good times this would make them and their homes look aesthetically pleasing and in bad times it would help them fend for themselves. Though a few women are earning a living these days as teachers, doctors and nurses, these are not suitable occupations in a culture like ours where ordinary women are confined to the limits of the *antahpur* [the inner quarters for women in a household]. Sometime ago we held a week-long 'Mahila Silpasamiti' conference at Rabindranath Tagore's house at 6 Dwarakanath Tagore Street, and arranged for the following types of training to be imparted there:

(i) Needlework—starting from simple threadwork to intricate designs with *jari*, silk, wool.
(ii) Work with knitting needles—knitting, crochet, tatting, making other kinds of laces and ribbons.
(iii) Machine work—sewing machine, knitting machine, embroidery machine. We had also arranged for weaving; women may not be able to weave on looms used for making saris but it might be possible for them to handle Assamese looms or those used by Bhutias to weave rugs.
(iv) Handicrafts—cutting, paper-making (for scrolls, etc), candle-making, pottery, wood carving and leather work.
(v) Fine Arts.
(vi) Music, songs and their notations.

The women were also taught how to spin threads from *charkas* [spinning wheels] at the first session. The trainees have promised to try and spin at least as much thread as required to weave a sari in a year's time. Some of them have requested that they be given some education as well. The education imparted to our women these days is not entirely suitable for them. We realize there is a need to educate them suitably but our financial resources are very meagre and we also do not have recourse to people who could teach them. So it is not possible to take on this task at present. We haven't been able to consolidate our efforts in the work already begun; god willing and with the help of our countrymen, if we succeed in this programme, we might be able to extend our work to educating women.

Our experience, however, tells us that it is perhaps not advisable to mix two kinds of training—one as a hobby and the other as a means of earning a livelihood. With this in mind we have made separate arrangements and divided our association's work. We are trying to set up a Nari Silpashala here [6 Dwarakanath Tagore Street] or at any other centrally located place in Calcutta where it would be possible to provide regular vocational training for women. Besides, we shall also explore setting up technical sections in association with a couple of girls' schools. There will be weekly sessions in five or six places all over Calcutta held at the residence of some of the women. These will be called Antahpur Kalabhavans. One must remember these Kalabhavans will be set up not with the sole aim of training in the arts. In the weekly sessions women will engage in art and crafts just as in a literary session people engage in reading. It is always more attractive to come to a forum and listen to people read than sit at home and read alone. Most women who will come to these sessions will be paying their bus fares not just to acquire skills but also to get a chance to meet others. Just as Sangeet Samaj is not simply a music school for men but a club to which they belong,[1] our Kalabhavans too would be clubs for women where they would also nurture their artistic aptitudes. Till now such sessions are being held only on Thursdays at 25 Lansdowne Road. We will try and see that such weekly meetings are organized in all the important neighbourhoods of the city. This will enable women to choose if they wish to attend more than one session. At these meetings women will teach each other arts and crafts and if necessary professionals will be appointed to teach cutting, tailoring and machine work in particular. It is not possible to train women from house-to-house at present.

We are grateful to Rabindranath Tagore for giving us permission to start the Nari Silpashala at his residence. It cannot be expected that all women from the antahpur will come together to acquire skills at the Kalabhavans. There are numerous problems that will keep them away—household work, looking after the children, conveyance and the like. But there is no doubt that through those who participate we shall be able to reach many others in the antahpur. We have noticed that women of a neighbourhood usually flock to someone in the vicinity who happens to be good with her hands because they want to learn from her. One of the main aims of the Silpashala would be to produce good art teachers. They would then be able to go house-to-house teaching women some skills.

In addition to the antahpur Kalabhavans and the Silpashala, we have taken on another task on behalf of the association: that is to inspire women to observe *matribratas* [the ritual observance of service to the motherland]. Our intention is not to keep this limited to members of our association but to spread this among all women in the city and the small towns. The purpose is to make the Indian woman realize that just as we have certain responsibilities towards our parents, siblings, husbands and children, we have responsibilities towards our motherland too. The ordinary women of our country are not used to meetings and speeches and do not respond particularly well to them. If we are to involve them, then we need to think of ways which appeal to them and which are feasible for them. Bengali women have long observed all kinds of *bratas*.[2] If they took to worshipping the motherland in the form of a brata, they would surely find it engaging. There are two parts to this brata: to start putting aside some coins or small amounts of money separately and to offer tributes in the form of handcrafted items. The first is to save a handful of money for the country every day and the second is to do some needlework or handwork from time to time. They are used to both kinds of work and love doing it. Here is an extraction from *Bharati* which carried an article on the usefulness of such a brata:

> A few women have vowed to observe a *brata* and called it *Lakhsmir Kouto*.[3] For this they do not have to do anything except save a handful of rice in the name of Annapurna, the Goddess of Plenty.[4] All they will have to do is place an earthen vessel or any vessel before the idol of Goddess Lakshmi and save daily at least a handful of rice for Bharatmata. It is so simple that no one should find it difficult. We pray that people realize the significance of observing this *brata* and start practising it. Not only will it raise funds for the nation but also help women teach their children an important lesson. If a mother teaches her child that after praying to God first thing in the morning, he or she should immediately afterwards pour in a handful of rice, for the sake of our motherland, in the vessel kept for the purpose, then the child is bound to be religious as well as patriotic. This is very important in the context of our country. In many countries they teach these values while children are being educated. But in our country it is just the opposite. A child will never forget the motherland if after being born into a patriotic family and fed on patriotism from the time he or she is breast-fed by the mother, knows the mother as well as the motherland from infancy, and learns to love fellow countrymen as deeply as siblings. No amount of indoctrination later will have a similar effect on him or her. We are indeed blessed and it is a miracle that today the wave of patriotism sweeping us is making us feel stronger than ever before. This is rare and just as a river sustains its banks as fresh and green forever, the lessons of childhood direct and influence our entire lives. If a mother sows the seeds of such an attitude in her child and if this is nurtured

and practised in the household, then the child will not waver from this belief even under the most severe pressures. On the contrary, the obstacles will make him/her more determined than ever. That is why I insist that such values should be imparted at home, and the concept of *Lakshmir Koutobrata* can only further this cause. Even before attaining the ability to reason, the child will be attracted to and influenced by this family tradition.

The woman who has vowed to observe the brata will thus reserve a few coins or a handful or two of rice every day for this purpose, and the donations gathered in this way could be donated towards the worship of the motherland on Poila Baisakh [15 April, the Bengali New Year], Bijoyadashami [the last day of the Durga Puja] or on a monthly basis. Each woman should also take it upon herself to induct another woman into this practice, which if established in every household then, just as Draupadi's pot of rice never ran out (she could feed thousands of people from a few remaining morsels[5]) the women will never lack reserves. These funds can be contributed for various projects such as support of some local handicrafts or to help a regional or national cause. It is the women, however, who have primary claim on these resources that they have put together, therefore most of them prefer to channel their contributions into supporting the work of Mahila Silpasamitis. Through this collection, arrangements could also be made for widows from the antahpur of respectable households to learn handicrafts, thus earning their own livelihood and lessening their sorrows.

The basis for national development is devotion to one's country. We pride ourselves on being devoted to our families, but until and unless we learn that the devotion we owe to our country is above what we owe to our families, the country will not prosper. Moreover this cannot be achieved by momentary enthusiasm—like a waterspout that suddenly spurts out powerfully towards the sky and then falls earthwards again, destroying everything it encounters. Sudden, momentary enthusiasm has much the same effect as the lava flow from a volcano that chars everything in its path. But consider the myriad small streams that spring from the depths of such mountains and join together on their way down to the plains—how much happiness and joy they bring us. If we want to generate patriotism for our country, we must lay a strong foundation for it. We must instil this attitude in every household—and the means for doing this are not the same for men and ourselves. We should concentrate on the lessons and values that can be imparted by virtue of living within the antahpur and through the daily domestic chores. I have spoken of one such instance, the *Lakshmir Kouto brata*. I now bring up another which is called 'Shilpanjali'. Whichever brata one decides to embrace, it should be followed with diligence—that is what 'brata' means.

In our country, all women are familiar with some form of handicrafts. If some of their spare time is used for this purpose and the material thus produced donated towards the nation, it would help our cause immeasurably. Many may ask, where do I have spare time in the midst of all the family chores? But what do 'family chores' entail? Looking after your parents, husband, children—the love and devotion we feel towards them has itself taught us our duty towards them. So if we felt a similar love and devotion for our country, we would automatically fulfil this additional duty as part of all our other 'family chores'. That we do not do it is owing to our short-sightedness; that is why our country's troubles do not cease, our children do not grow into well-rounded human beings. That is why, by society at large, they are looked down upon as inferior and weak. If we are to develop our children into adult human beings, we must instil this sense of love and devotion towards the country in them. But if the mothers themselves do not experience this love towards the motherland, how are they going to pass on this feeling to their children? In the span of 24 hours if we are not able to spare even half an hour or 15 minutes to devote to some activity which will help the nation in some way, if we are hesitant to commit ourselves for our country's sake, how will our children imbibe the sense of staking all they have for the motherland? And who will this work on our part benefit in reality? Will it not be for the sake of our children? Poor parents go without food themselves in order to be able to bear the cost of educating their sons, but it is simply because we have not learnt that institutional education does not transform a child into a well-rounded adult, that we do not make attempts to instil other forms of learning in them.

We must understood that all kinds of learning are equally important; spiritual teachings and a sense of patriotism contribute immensely to the *Lakshmir Kouto* and Shilpanjali, and are so simple that they will not hinder any woman in any way when she takes them up. I have described the former at length already. The second is as follows: a woman begins to make something using whichever craft or art form she is comfortable with, and reserves half an hour or 15 minutes a day to work on it. After completion she sells it and after having deducted what she would need to start on another similar (or different) piece of work, donates the remainder of the amount to some worthy cause in the interest of the nation. This is how this project will continue.

The women of the Samiti who choose to become involved in Shilpanjali will be provided with the necessary materials from the Samiti. And the money that will be collected after the sale of items will be spent in the work of the Narishilpashala. Here, it is necessary to state the following with regard to Shilpanjali. Today, since many people will not use foreign materials, they have given up their crafts as local materials are not always readily available. When it is necessary for this inculcation, we should include both the indigenous and the foreign. If our women had not ceased to work on their arts and crafts, we would not be lacking local materials today. The women of Bombay are skilled in arts and crafts—a lot of indigenous materials are found there. There are efforts on to make local materials available here as well, but in the meantime, why refuse to use things foreign if these are not available locally?

This year all those who have chosen to take the Shilpanjali brata have been provided with new materials. Next year, another scheme will also be implemented along with this. Old and used clothes will be collected, cut up and sewn to make them usable. These will then be distributed amongst the poor, specifically to young boys and girls.

The Samiti has one more objective: because of a mandate on using only Swadeshi goods, we have suddenly had to come face to face with many problems, two of which are experienced most acutely by women; we must try to remedy this. One of them is that since we no longer know where essential everyday items are to be procured, a lot of time and effort is spent in getting them. The Samiti will prepare a list of where items are available so that women will easily be able to procure whatever is necessary. We are also faced with the unavailability of one other item: toys. Indigenous toys have all but disappeared and even what is available is obtained with the greatest difficulty. The Samiti will try and make some new toys and also arrange to collect toys from various places. There will be a weekly meeting for teaching women art and craft. Besides, all the women of Calcutta will be invited to the Samiti's quarterly meetings where there will be presentations of music and recitation apart from the sale of toys and items collected from the Shilpanjali programme. There will be a display of articles of daily use and women weavers and confectioners will be invited to bring their wares.

All the schemes that the Samiti is trying to implement are dependent on funds, and the money that comes in through observance of *matribrata* and from contributions of a few women will not be much. In particular, we need a lot of money for setting up the Narishilpashala. We earnestly request all people who wish to see our country prosper to contribute in any small way to this cause.

Translated by Sarmistha Dutta Gupta

From 'প্রস্তাব: শিল্পসমিতি বা মহিলাশিল্পসমিতি', ভান্ডার, খন্ড ১, সংখ্যা ১২, চৈত্র, ১৩১২ বঙ্গাব্দ, মার্চ-এপ্রিল, ১৯০৪।

'Prostab: Shilpasamiti ba Mahilashilpasamiti', *Bhandar*, vol 1, issue 12, Chaitra, 1312 B.S., March-April, 1904.

Notes

1 Founded by Jyotirindranath Tagore, the author's maternal uncle. See also 16, Sarala Devi, 'My Life Changes Track', n18, this volume.
2 Folk rituals performed by women who take a vow for the fulfilment of a particular desire that requires fasting and steadfast observance.
3 Lakhsmi, the Goddess of Wealth, is imagined iconically as carrying a *kouto* (casket) that is always full.
4 The Mother Goddess who provides food for the family.
5 The *Mahabharata* relates that Draupadi, exiled in the forest with her five husbands, was blessed by the Sun God with a magic utensil which would fill up with food, thus enabling her to provide for unexpected guests.

13   Khairunnissa Khatun

It is very difficult to find information about Khairunnissa Khatun who undertook pioneering work in the education of Muslim girls in purdah. She was married to Moulana Asiruddin. It is known that she died between 1908 (when the first edition of her book, Satir Patibhakti *was published) and 1911 (at the time of the reprint when she was no longer alive). She set up a 'night school' which could be attended by girls who would then come into contact with fewer men. She was born and lived in Pabna (today in Bangladesh) and ran Shirazgunj Hossainpur Girls School, of which she was the principal.*[1] *A staunch opponent of the Partition of Bengal, 1905, she was very active in the Swadeshi movement, participating in rallies and conventions organized by the Indian National Congress, which brought her criticism from the more orthodox Muslims.*

Patriotism

The various debates and agitations currently taking place in Bengal are proving to be beneficial for our fallen country. There is no doubt that the Partition of Bengal is the root cause.[2] Today, in each and every village and town—aristocrats, lawyers and clerks, the educated and the illiterate—all are organizing huge rallies and are vowing to repudiate foreign goods. At this time what should be the attitude of their womenfolk? In this essay I wish to say a few words about that.

Sisters, do we have no right to worry about the things to which our fathers, brothers and husbands have dedicated their minds and bodies? The things that occupy all their time, and attention? Indeed, we have just as much right! If we don't give them appropriate help, if we do not express sympathy for their struggles, would that not show disrespect for their affection towards us and bring discredit to our role as the better halves of our husbands? I have no doubt that it will do so.

We should not sit silently during this time of great upheaval. It is our duty to join in and offer what help we can. I am not suggesting that you organize a great assembly, nor am I suggesting you gather on street corners or at the Town Hall to listen to speeches. If we so desire, we can sit in one corner of the room and assist the menfolk. The assistance is nothing more than making a few sacrifices about a few things. Sisters, if your sacrifices benefit our motherland, if your sacrifice leads to the wealth and prosperity of our country, if your sacrifice leads to the reappearance of lost crafts, then why should you be averse to making them? And why would you cringe from the pain that the sacrifice may entail? Come, let us be as resolute as the men and show society that India can be helped by women and through their efforts great welfare may arise. Sisters, we all remember the sacrifice of Kshatriya women who in order to help their men had relinquished their valuable and much adored jewellery encrusted with precious stones. They sold their clothes embroidered with gold threads. They did not even hesitate to shear their glorious hair so that it could be used as bowstrings. Why should we be so hesitant in making some small sacrifices? If today, despite being the immediate helpmeets of our men, we refuse to offer them our help and encouragement, will not God curse us?

Sisters, come let us be steadfast in our resolve to relinquish foreign saris; and let us look at bodices [blouses], chemises and socks with contempt. Instead of lavender let us learn to use rose attar[3] and by giving up wearing ladies' shoes prevent ourselves from stumbling. Then we will benefit our country a great deal. In Bombay, Dhaka, Pabna, Nadia, Murshidabad and other places different sorts of fabric: dhotis, silk saris and embroidered materials [chikon] are produced. These fabrics are lustrous and they are durable. If we use them our money will remain in our country, our domestic industry will improve, and poor weavers and labourers will be able to work and provide for themselves. The improvement of our society depends on the efforts of our womenfolk. I suppose the efforts of the men are not as effective. If we prohibit foreign goods from entering our homes, will the men be able to bring them in? We have a greater hold on the home. If some man is partial to foreign goods, then cannot our pleading be successful in weaning him off them? Of course, it is possible! If not, then in what sense are we the better halves?

In our country, much jute and silk are produced but we don't know how to value them. Foreigners buy them for a song and then we are made to buy foreign cloth at exorbitant prices. If we bought domestically produced cloth, then we could build our own factories here at home and then the jute and silk produced in our own country could be used here. Foreigners must not load up their ships with our wealth and set sail across the oceans and devastate our country.

And look, how awful it has been since the introduction of enamelled utensils. We had been using utensils made of brass, copper and other metals. Out of the blue, these glossy yet easily breakable pots and pans have filled our homes. Even when our domestic metal utensils break, we are able to sell them for half the price. But sisters, have you even seen the broken enamel pots fetching any price at all? When a householder is in financial trouble, if he has some brass and copper pots and pans he can make some money by selling or pawning them, for these are still considered valuable property. But enamel is not cheap either. Since these are household objects, if we don't use them, surely our menfolk will not be able to force us to use them. Come, sisters, let us vow that we will not touch enamel. Let us see whether we can reintroduce the use of metal pots and pans.

Do you not notice, sisters, that we are on the road to disaster. If we were not gullible would the traders have come from across the seven seas to deceive us with inferior German silver jewellery and fancy bangles and then fill up their ships with Bharat's wealth and riches? And we delude ourselves by believing we are acquiring valuable goods! Are not these at the root of our downfall? If we were to think sensibly it would not be an exaggeration to say that foreigners are in a way looting us. India can provide all commodities to the world—in other words, whatever is available in the rest of the world can be found in this country. And living in such a country why are we, day by day, descending towards ruination? Have you paused to give this even a passing thought?

Realizing that we are a naive lot, traders from America, England, Scotland, Germany, Australia, Switzerland and Japan, among other nations, continually take all that we produce through hard labour in exchange for trivial things. We are reduced to begging from door to door for a bite to eat. Until we are able to escape the lure of these traders we will continue on the road to ruin.

Many in our country keep one or two cows for the purpose of drinking milk. Almost all gentlemen drink milk daily. Nonetheless, it is as if without imported tinned milk we do not like the taste of tea. What a calamity! Just thinking about this makes one depressed. When a country is on the brink of disaster, its condition becomes lamentable. Sisters, you drink tea, and declaring tinned milk pure, feed it to infants. But do you even pause to wonder whether the milk is from donkeys or from horses? It is only in this wretched country that imported milk that comes from overseas is considered better than the fresh milk produced at home. Surely, no one else would think this way.

Molasses, sugar, unrefined sugar are produced in abundant quantities in our country. Before the arrival of the British, Indians were satisfied with these. Now we are contemptuous about consuming domestic molasses and sugar. We can't do without refined sugar. We find our sugar and molasses full of impurities. Each year we import some five and a half crores [fifty-five million] rupees worth of refined sugar into this country. Sisters, if five and a half crores stayed in the country, would it not do a lot of good? We give these matters little thought. If we so wanted, could we not refine our domestic molasses? We surely can, so come, let us begin consuming Swadeshi molasses and sugar.

There is another dangerous trend towards which a good deal of our money is being diverted: cigarettes and cheroots. We grow quite good tobacco in our country. But our school and college students are much more attracted to foreign cigarettes. I have no idea why they are so attracted. In my opinion it is probably a part of behaving like a babu. These tobacco products account for thirty lakhs of rupees going abroad. If this money were utilized to harvest domestic tobacco and other essential ingredients, we would benefit greatly. A lot of money would remain in the country.

Sisters, our children are smoking poisonous foreign cigarettes which are destroying their health. And do we pay any attention to that? It is lamentable that despite being concerned mothers we remain uncertain, encouraging rather than forbidding our children from using these poisonous substances. If we tried, could we not rescue our children from these harmful substances? If we strictly forbade our children from touching these dangerous cigarettes, would they defy us? Do mother's injunctions have no value?

Dear Sisters, today a few topics have been mentioned. It is to be hoped that each of us will try her very best to improve the lot of our country. If you remain oblivious, what will happen to our poor country? It is time to wake up. If we still looked around, our efforts would accomplish much.

Translated by Modhumita Roy

From 'স্বদেশানুরাগ', *নবনূর*, আশ্বিন, ১৩১২ বঙ্গাব্দ, সেপ্টেম্বর-অক্টোবর, ১৯০৫।

'Swadeshanurag', *Nabanur*, Aswin, 1312 B.S., Sept-Oct, 1905.

Notes

1 She would beg that a handful of uncooked rice be set aside before the rice was cooked, which she would collect to sell and raise money for her school. She said the following on the status of women in the family: *(i)* the root cause of degeneration of society is the low position

of women; *(ii)* the family where women are oppressed is destroyed; *(iii)* women are meant for many purposes, not only to be mothers; *(iv)* the family where the husband is content with his wife prospers; and *(v)* behind every husband's great work is a wife who it treated with respect.
2 See 9, Kumudini Mitra, 'What Women Should Do When the Motherland Is in Distress', n1.
3 Concentrated perfume, prepared from roses in the Mughal period.

14 Jagadishwari Devi

Nothing at all is known about Jagadishwari Devi except that she wrote this piece in Bharat Mahila, *1908.*

On the Use of Footwear by Women in Ancient India

When I was young I once visited Chandimandap [a place where Durga is worshipped] at the time of the Durga Puja with my aunt. I saw that lying next to the priest there were an expensive sari, conch bangles, a small silver seat and ring, a brass pot filled with curd, a mirror, a comb, *alta* [the red dye that was used to paint the feet], a small box of sindoor, an umbrella, a bed, *kharam* [wooden clogs] and shoes. I asked my aunt, 'Why have these things—a sari, bangles, shoes—been kept here?' She replied, 'These are for the Goddess.' I said, 'But the Goddess is a woman, if she can wear shoes, why can't we?' My aunt shuddered and said, 'You foolish girl, she is a Goddess. The Gods can do what they like, but does that mean that human beings can do the same things?' I wasn't satisfied with this explanation.

Three years ago I went on a pilgrimage to Puri and Bhubaneswar, and at a famous temple in Bhubaneswar, I saw a number of human figures carved out of stone. Some of them were of women, and their feet were shod in footwear that resembled boots. I showed them to a holy man who had accompanied me. 'Look, the women are wearing shoes.' He said, 'In ancient times, such as in Satyayug, women were permitted to wear shoes, but with the onset of Kaliyug, it has been forbidden.'

I laughed and recited:

'*gajashtemite jate shakabde krittibasasya
prasadam kurute raja shri lalatendu keshari.*'[1]

'Look, this verse is inscribed on the temple. It proves that the temple was built in 588 shakabda (A.D. 666). Had not Kaliyug started then?'

My companion smiled and said, 'What's the use of arguing? If you want to wear shoes, you are free to do so, I don't mind.'

Perhaps because of this he bought me a pair of shoes when we reached Kurseong. There was no difficulty in wearing them in the lonely mountain tops, but I feared that two months of use would make it a habit. After my return to my crowded homeland I might become addicted, and want to wear it someday and be ostracized as a result. So I did not wear them at all.

I read in our ancient texts that Padmini, the queen of the ill-fated king Jayachandra, made the philosopher and poet Sriharsha put shoes on her feet.[2] In the description of Mahasweta's hermitage in the *Kadambari* we read[3]:

*vishakhika shikharanibaddha narikelaphalabalkalamaya
dhoutopadena yugalopetam . . . grham adraskshit.*[4]

Some scholars interpret *vishakhika* as a long pole placed inside the house; others as a log of wood, with or without branches. Whatever it might be, there are a pair of shoes tied to the top of it, made of the fibre of the coconut, properly washed: in those days even recluses like Mahasweta wore shoes, now it is forbidden even to women leading domestic lives. One does not know the reason for this. I think it is for the same reason that European beauties leave the better part of their bosom uncovered that Indian women have given up wearing shoes. Otherwise the pleasure gained by men at the sight of those dainty feet, resembling young plants, adorned with silver ornaments, tinged with alta, would not have been achieved. Neither would women have professed their subjection to their cream-like feet. I do not know whether God will ever free women from their present fate, where they are merely lifeless puppets, objects of household decoration.

Translated by Amlan Dasgupta

From 'প্রাচীন ভারতে নারীজাতির উপানৎ ব্যবহার', ভারত মহিলা,
চৈত্র, ১৩১৬ বঙ্গাব্দ, মার্চ-এপ্রিল, ১৯০৮।

'Prachin Bharat Narijatir Upanat Byabahar', *Bharat Mahila*,
Chaitra, 1316 B.S., March-April, 1908.

Notes

1 The inscription on the temple says that in the specified year Raja Lalatendukeshari ordered the temple to be built to please Lord Shiva (Krittibash).
2 Sriharsha, who is primarily known for his *Naishadacharitam*, was a court poet of the twelfth century, whose patron was King Jayachandra of Kanauj.
3 Mahasweta is one of the heroines of the prose romance, *Kadambari*, written by the poet Banabhatta who lived in the seventh century.
4 'Saw a house in which there was a pole, tied to the top of which was a pair of sandals made of coconut fibre, properly washed.'

15   Swarnakumari Devi

Swarnakumari Devi (1855–1932) was the daughter of Debendranath Tagore and Sarada Devi and the older sister of Rabindranath, and thus a member of the Jorasanko Tagore family that was famed for its brilliant intellectual and cultural achievements. Swarnakumari herself was amongst its most gifted members, excelling as a poet, a novelist, a literary editor and as a committed social worker who founded Sakhi Samiti to help widows and destitute women. Indeed she 'heralded a new era for women'.[1] *At 13 she was married to Janakinath Ghosal, a deputy magistrate, who later became closely involved with the nationalist movement and Swarnakumari was one of the few women who attended the Indian National Congress's conference at Bombay in 1889. Among her novels are* Deepnirban, Snehalata, Kahake, *and* Phuler Mala. *She wrote two plays,* Bibaha Utsav *and* Pakchakra. *Her poems were collected in* Gatha, Kabita o Gaan *and her songs in* Geetiguccha. *She received the Jagattarini Gold Medal from the University of Calcutta.*

Words from Times Past

The relationship of the former editor of *Bharati* with Manilal Ganguly is both sour and sweet. He has married my granddaughter, and is thus a grandson-in-law.[2] When food becomes unpalatable, it is the taste of something sour that brings back the appetite. He has been very persuasive, 'You must write of the times past.' This gentle request from the new editor has eased even the bitter task of writing, and the responsibility of penning down words also seems lighter today.

Do I have to write of the times past? Oh, really! I have already become a part of the past! If I do not repeat this constantly, I tend to forget it. It was only the other day when our poor grandmothers would be fed-up with our present-day behaviour, and we, the new women, would very easily bear with their old-time reproaches and feel as proud as heroines.

By right of being older, the very potent weapon of reproach is our prerogative today, yet instead of using it we thought it best to keep it under lock and key. The winds of evolution have gathered so much strength that not only the Women's Suffrage group in England, but also women's groups and societies all over the world are impatient to gain their rights.[3] Modern Bangla literature proves quite positively that the Bengali woman too is not weak anymore. Of course, I am quite afraid that she will soon stop me by taking away my weapon. I know very well that if I try to blame her, she will say, '"today" was brought into being by "yesterday", so you alone are responsible for our deeds.'

True enough, but then what insolence! Could we have answered in a similar manner in our days? Our hearts would burst and still our lips would remain sealed. So you see, the more equipped the girls are today to express and to understand, the less their capacity to sustain and to endure. In brief, that is the main sign of this age. Good health, labour, normal delivery are now counted as fashions of bygone days. There is nothing else apart from this that I can think of saying. What was not there in our times is still non-existent. It is the seeds and the saplings of the past that are now in full bloom. But the tree that has withered and the flower that has fallen are yet to be replaced.

Of women's education I can say this that although the B.A.s and M.A.s that you now have did not exist then, yet learned women were even at that time held in high esteem. At least that is the example I saw in my family. And it was in our days that the foundation of modern methods for the education of women was laid.

What I wrote many years back in a journal called *Pradip* regarding education in the *antahpur* [the women's rooms around the inner quarters of the house, also referred to as 'inner house'] may be new to many now.⁴ With this hope and faith I shall relate what I had promised and conclude this essay.

It is almost a century since my mother came to our house as a bride. Then my great grandfather's family had filled our antahpur. Grandfather Dwarakanath Tagore and his brothers and sisters were all living with their families in one house.⁵ It is said that no woman in these families was illiterate. On the contrary, there were a few who were particularly learned and therefore respected. Even then they took pride in women's education.

This then is what the past was like for me. And the trend continues even to our day. I have seen a distant relative, a cousin sister of my mother's age, writing in excellent flawless Bangla. She also had some knowledge of Sanskrit. So she was respected not only among the women, but among the male members in the family as well. Indeed, I have not encountered such respect for education in their grandchildren. Some were even illiterate. The young women of the next generation perhaps did not find the same atmosphere of learning and education that had nurtured the old and the elderly ladies in our family.

Studies, along with food, recreation and worship, were a daily ritual among women in our antahpur. As the milkmaid came every morning with her milk, the all-knowing priest with his almanac to talk about the auspicious and the inauspicious on the quotidian level, so also, after her holy bath, the white-clad, fair-complexioned lady Vaishnavi would appear in the antahpur to disseminate the light of learning.⁶ Her intellect and learning were extraordinary. Quite well-versed in Sanskrit, she evidently knew Bangla well. Moreover, she had an excellent flair for descriptions and she would enchant everyone with her art of storytelling. Even those who did not wish to acquire knowledge would be curious to listen to lady Vaishnavi's descriptions of Gods and Goddesses and of the dawn and would thus gather round her. I did not have the good fortune to meet lady Vaishnavi and so I do not have a first-hand knowledge of her descriptive abilities. But for the appreciation of the new generation I quote from memory her description of the dawn as narrated by my aunt.

'The night is far advanced, but cannot bid farewell; dawn has arrived at the edge of the eastern horizon, but is unable to make herself visible, for Sri Krishna and Radhika are sleeping locked in each other's arms in an embrace of love. Poor lovers, they have spent the whole night pacifying each other and so in the early hours of the morning they have fallen into a deep sleep. Oh, look! Oh, the heaven and the earth, the entire cosmos is struck motionless at the meeting of Radhika, the symbol of love, with Sri Hari, her life's breath. The night birds are silent; the streams and rivers are bereft of current, animals, men and women are in deep sleep, the morning star is unable to set in the eastern sky and the Sun God on his golden chariot is afraid of making his appearance. Chaos is about to overtake creation. The Sun God in anxiety turns his chariot and comes to the door of Brahma and tells him of the impending disaster. Brahma silently takes note of the danger and sinks in meditation. After meditating he still cannot find any solution and so he calls Krishna's bird Rampakkhi [the cock]. When the bird arrives, he says, "O bird, devotee of Krishna, only you can save us from this danger. O the last resort of the resortless, the devotee of devotees, who else but you can dare to disturb the sleep of Vishnu? So taking mercy upon Gods and Goddesses, men and rakshasas, go and wake him—or else the whole of creation will now be lost." The bird, satisfied with the words of Brahma, reassures him, goes to the door of Vrindavana and calls out—"Kukkuhuk" or 'Wake up, do!"—"Kukkuhuk! Kukkuhuk!" Sri Krishna opens his lotus eyes and sees that it is dawn.

'As far as I remember Sri Krishna was not ashamed. On the other hand, for the sin of interrupting his joyful amorous union, he cursed the bird. It is because of the curse that the holy venerable cock of ancient days is now untouchable to the Hindu and the food of non-Hindus.'

It is not as if I have recited the entire story in the language of my aunt—no doubt it has been transformed. It was as a very small child that I would pester my aunt for the story. With all my heart and all my soul I would wait for the word 'Kukkuhuk'. I would not pay attention to the first part because I would be waiting impatiently for the bird to call out. But I have heard the story so often that it is possible for me to remember and to reconstruct it now.

The Vaishnavi would come for the ladies confined within the four walls of the antahpur; newly wed young wives and young married daughters of the house would receive their education from her. But the young unmarried daughters of the house would go along with the boys to the village school or pathshala run by the guru. This at least, if nothing else, laid a similar foundation for the education of both boys and girls.

That was before the time of Vidyasagar's *Barnaparichay*.[7] The lady Vashnavi used a booklet called *Sishubodhak* to teach the letters of the alphabet, which I came across when I grew up. This single booklet taught everything from letters and spellings to invocations of Gods and Goddesses, to descriptions of various hours of the day and methods of writing. The language of invocations and descriptions was so difficult and obscure, that if one could read and understand it one would, in a way, complete the learning process of Bangla. First they would practice writing on palm leaves and then on banana leaves. The process of writing with pens of bamboo twig on coarse paper came last.

In my childhood everyone in the antahpur betrayed a love for learning. My mother would always have a book in her hand during her leisure hours. A special favourite of hers was the *Chanakyasloka*— she would often take the book and repeat the *slokas*. One of my brothers would frequently be called to read out the Sanskrit *Ramayana* and *Mahabharata* to her. My grandmother—mother's paternal aunt—was a real bookworm. Of course, there were the novels and poetic works; but she would not rest until she had tried the most complex translations of *Tantrapurana, Samkhya* or other philosophic texts. If she did not find any other book she would take the dictionary and sit down with it. There was no one else who understood my elder brother's *Tattvavidya* as she did.[8] My aunts, sisters and the newly-wed young women, of course, preferred novels. Ever since I learnt to read I was assigned the special task of reading out the *Ramayana,* the *Mahabharata* and *Hatemtai* to our aunt. I remember what excitement there was in the women's wing when the flower-woman came to sell books. She brought all the new books—poems, novels and tall tales—from Battala—and increased the size of the library in our antahpur. As there would be cupboards full of dolls, toys, clothes, and so on, so also there would be chests full of books in every household. As I grew older, I had the occasion to shuffle through those books of times past— *Manbhanjan, Probhasmilon, Dutisambad, Kokilduta, Rukminiharan, Parijatharan, Geetgovinda, Prahladcharitra, Rotibilap, Bastraharan, Annadamangal, The Arabian Tales* and *The Persian Tales* in Bangla, *Chahardarbesh, Hatemtai, Gul-e-b-quawali, Layla Majnun, Basabdatta, Kaminikumar,* and so on. The reader can well see that only one out of all these books has a title with a social bearing; *Kaminikumar* is a novel written in verse. Novels in prose had not been written at that time.

Much later, during our childhood, Ramnarayan Tarkaratna, after having translated Sanskrit plays in prose, composed social plays such as *Kulinkulasarvasya, Bahubibaha Natak* and so forth.[9] Kaliprasanna Sinha's *Hutom Pyanchar Naksha* and Pyari Chand Mitra's novels[10] came even later. Yet why could I not find *Kaminikumar*'s name in the list of literary works? *Kaminikumar* is a novel in verse, but it is unique in that it did not really imitate *Vidyasundar,* for earlier Bharatchandra would always figure as the model for 'Kavya' literature.[11] It has been stated that when Madanmohan Tarkalankar started writing *Basabdatta,* he vowed to outdo Bharatchandra even while imitating him.[12] But when his book came out he was heartbroken at the verdict of the connoisseurs and in frustration he consigned his beloved *Basabdatta* to the flames. Madanmohan's fame remained confined to the few books he had published before.

I can hardly say that the poetic or the novelistic value of *Kaminikumar* is great—yet it deserves a place in the history of literature. It is the first text where men and women from contemporary Bengali society are the protagonists. As far as I can remember the story of *Kaminikumar* goes like this—there is first an account of the nayaka and the nayika, then a description of their beauty followed by their meeting as they grow into adults and fall in love with each other. Next they set out on a journey hoping to meet each other. The places where they travel are described and they meet several times. Kamini is disguised as a man and is therefore a stranger to Kumar, but Kamini recognizes Kumar and engages him in a tantalizing conversation. Eventually both return home, meet and get married. The writer is Girindranath Tagore, my second eldest uncle.[13]

My father was known both as a pious man and a religious reformer.[14] And since in our country religious and social customs are not separate but linked together, a certain degree of social reform inevitably follows religious reform. My father was also known, to a lesser extent, as a social reformer. But this was not undertaken as a less important task. We alone can bear testimony to the fact that he was devoted to social reform in the same manner as he was to religious reform. It was he who laid the foundation of higher education for women and was the first to bring in reform in the sphere of child marriage as well as in matters such as the introduction of civilized clothes for women. In religious reform Rammohan Roy's name precedes others, but it would not be an exaggeration to say that in Bengal, my father was the pioneer of social reform. My father was among those who disregarded social criticism and sent his daughters to Bethune School soon after its establishment.[15] Educational reforms in the antahpur stopped completely after my father left for the hills. It was only when he returned that things truly began to change for the better. It was then that both religious and educational reform gained momentum.

The first thing my father did after returning was to do away with the *salgramsila* [the black stone that represents the God Narayana] and convert the entire family to Brahmoism. Every day he would talk about true religion at the time of worship, and at other times he would speak in a simple and lucid manner on various scientific topics and thus cater to the equal refinement of the intellect, knowledge and religious sensibility of his family members, especially of the antahpur. He was not just satisfied with removing idolatry; gradually he also did away with long-standing and debasing women's rituals in our antahpur. These were prevalent in the whole of India. He fixed a particular age for the marriage of young girls, though lower than what is the custom today, and initiated a new method for marriage ceremonies. Our family, right from the marriage of my second sister, has followed the same wedding customs. When his daughters became old enough to receive education, they began to be taught through a superior and upgraded method. A Sanskrit teacher was appointed for us. We finished our second primer and began to study Sanskrit along with Bangla. A European lady began to come to the antahpur.

Keshab babu became my father's disciple while these innovations were taking place in our family.[16] This was the first time that someone who was not a relative was allowed to enter the antahpur that was untouched by the sun and be welcomed like a very close relative. Many witnessed in this incident an act of great courage and were surprised. But was it all that surprising that my venerable father, who had not hesitated to sacrifice friends and relatives, comforts and pleasures for the sake of religion, should reject social norms and welcome Keshab babu as a son to his house? Keshab babu who had been thrown out of his house for embracing the true religion and who had come as a disciple with his wife to take shelter in my father's house?

What surprises one is something else that came later. All that I have said so far relates to the time prior to the departure of my second brother [Satyendranath Tagore] for England.[17] A few years after he left for England a gentleman not related to the family gained access to the antahpur. My father did not think that the English lady's method of teaching had produced the desired results. A new acharya of the Adi Brahmo Samaj, Ayodhyanath Pakrashi, was appointed teacher in the antahpur.[18] My third brother, Hemendranath Tagore, was already married by then.[19] The wives of my three brothers, my aunt, my elder sister and we three younger sisters studied with her. We studied arithmetic, Sanskrit, history and geography in English from school textbooks.

One could not wear a single sari, the usual dress of the Bengali lady, before a stranger and so on this occasion, there was a dress reform in the antahpur [see 8, Hemantakumari Chaudhuri, 'Women's Dress', this volume]. My elder sister, our aunt and my sisters-in-law would go to study attired in a pretty peshowaj [baggy pyjamas worn by women in north India] and a long scarf. My father had a lifelong distaste for the attire of the Bengali woman and wanted to bring about its reform. He put his wishes into practice by constantly experimenting with his young daughters and occasionally with his sisters. In those days children in our house would wear clothes similar to those worn by children in aristocratic Muslim families. But when we grew a little older we would frequently dress ourselves in new costumes. Our father would look at pictures and order our clothes; the tailor would come to him every day and so would we. Yet, in spite of all these tests, he failed to find a dress which really satisfied him. He was satisfied only when my second brother's wife [Jnanadanandini] came back from Bombay dressed in the pretty and befitting manner of Gujarati ladies. This dress, by combining tradition, taste and propriety, gave him exactly what he had wanted and by catering to a long and deeply felt need of the Bengali woman, gratified his long-standing wish.

After returning from England my second brother, Satyendranath, began to work in earnest on projects dealing with the uplift of women. It was not as if he had been silent and inactive in this sphere all these days, but then the son had been helping the father who provided leadership, and now having become independent and capable, he installed himself in his father's place after his retirement. Since his childhood he was a friend of women, in favour of women's education and women's freedom. Indeed before going abroad he had published a book justifying the women's cause with substantial arguments.[20] Most of the unconventional work that my father undertook for the welfare of the inner house was inspired and suggested by him. He was like my father's right hand in all these activities and he would also constantly try to induce my mother to improve the condition of the inner house.[21] When he became independent and capable he tried with an unfailing enthusiasm to translate into practice the ideal that he had cherished and nurtured in his heart as a kind of vow ever since he was born. From now onwards, not only in our house, but in Bengali society itself, it was the beginning of his era. The father had laid the foundation for women's higher education, the son built a castle on it; the father had planted a sapling in his antahpur that the son very carefully brought to fruition, distributing its product in society. The father became a pioneer in Bengal by introducing reforms at home, while it gratified the son to hand over to others the example of the household. One was the progenitor of higher education for women, the other a pioneer of women's freedom.

My second brother returned from England at the end of 1864 and started working from 1865. The tradition of keeping women confined to the inner house was very much in force then. At that time, even when women were going from one house to another in the same courtyard, there would be an accompanying guard running along with the fully covered palanquin. Then if mother, after a lot of entreaties and supplications, did get the permission to go and bathe in the Ganges, the palanquin bearers would take her, dip the palanquin into the water, and bring her back. My second brother took his wife to Bombay by sea, but even then he could not get her to walk to the car from the antahpur to the outer courtyard. For a lady of the house it was so new, so shameful, that the entire household voiced its disapproval. And so eventually she went in a palanquin and boarded the ship. A French lady designed the new dress that she would wear outside.

But even destiny succumbs to the tide of invincible desire—why speak of man? When my brother returned home with his wife after two years, no one could ask her to come home in a palanquin. Yet the sorrow that was expressed at the sight of a lady of the house getting off a car at the main gate is beyond description.

During this period they lived in a kind of segregation even within the house. The other women in the house were afraid of eating and drinking and even of mixing freely with my sister-in-law. But several years later when my brother returned from Bombay the second time, there was less rigidity. I had just been married at that time. My husband too, acting in accordance with his faith in the uplift and education of women, had to suffer a great deal in life.[22] He joined my brother wholeheartedly, thus strengthening his position and bringing about a great change of opinion in many members of the family.

In 1873 when I was fourteen my husband left me in Bombay for my education. I hardly knew any English then; I had learnt just a little. I was there with my daughter Hiranmoyee for a year.[23] We returned home together at the end of that year.

The river banks of conservatism that had started eroding caved in over a large area. On returning to Calcutta, my brother was no longer isolated, but found many others on his side. Gradually within a few days the atmosphere in the house changed completely.

It is important at this point to mention the relentless encouragement and endeavour on the part of my third brother, Hemendranath, for the education of the younger family members, and he was someone who had not talked about women's independence. Before his marriage he would often teach us himself. After his marriage he concentrated his efforts on his wife. He was the first to break traditional norms and make his wife [Neepomoyee] take music lessons from Bishnu, a regular singer in our house.[24] Maharshi also did not disapprove of this. Pratibha Devi, who stands in the front rank of Bengali ladies proficient in music, is Hemendranath's daughter.[25] My husband too appointed an ustad to teach me to play the sitar when I returned from Bombay and we began to live on our own.

It was from this time that gradually education began to gain more importance in our house. Young children were well taught in the spheres of music and education. Even my sisters began to learn English in a rigorous manner at home. It was no longer discreditable to travel by car, and palanquins were more or less discarded. It is about half a century now since my second brother returned from England and during this period through his efforts and example a vast change has taken place in our inner house.

And why just talk about our house? My brother Satyendranath's example has spread to the whole of Bengal. It is no more as embarrassing or as novel for a respectable lady to go out of her house. There is no dearth of civilized garments to put on and face the world.

Women's education and women's independence have spread far and wide. The thorny path which Satyendranath cleared and broadened is now simply and easily available to any Bengali woman. Leave aside the advanced ones—the stream of progress flows through the inmates of the antahpur as well. Now the bridegroom's family, while coming to see the bride, asks about the daughter's level of education at the very beginning. The pursuit of education in earnest, daughter-like behaviour even with parents-in-law, travel by car, dressing in accordance with the fashion of Bombay—are all now a part of Hindu social norms. And fifty years back the one who initiated this reform had to move forward by throwing aside a hundred hindrances single-handedly. Some family members were afraid of joining him. Yet he was so firmly resolved in ameliorating the condition of women, and received such joy from thoughts of women's well-being, that in his single-minded, concentrated strivings he did not acknowledge any hindrance, nor did he bend down to any insult. Even today there are men who feel ashamed at being singled out as people who have brought one or two women with them to a social occasion attended overwhelmingly by men. Moreover, they do not introduce their wives to those belonging to a different group, that is, to those men who do not take their wives out. My brother's feelings and beliefs were totally against such an attitude and if someone raised the issue, he would say, 'Why shouldn't I take one or two women to a gathering where many men will be present? How will those who do not take their wives out learn if we do not bring our wives before them? How will they change their habits?' Those were not just words, for he acted accordingly. It was not possible to invite him alone to formal or to informal gatherings. Everybody knew that if the women of the house were not invited, he would not come. Respect for women was such an integral part of my brother's character that it was impossible for him to think of any respectable gentleman looking at women with disrespect.

If you were to tell my brother that men are intellectually superior to women, if you were to say that higher education as in the case of men is unnecessary for women, that in the domain of work they are not equal to men, he would at once take up the cause of women and start arguing with passion. If the women in the household wanted to go to the museum, to the zoo or to attend a lecture and no male escort was available, my brother, if he got to hear of it, would take them to the desired destination in spite of his inconvenience or disability. He would be the advocate if the women wanted to make an appeal to the head of the family; the women of the family knew that there was no friend like Mejodada [second eldest brother], no support comparable with his and their trust in him was infinite. Actually it was rare to find such a devoted well-wisher of women, one who could act as their leader and one who was endowed with such a large, open and magnanimous soul. I would not be able to say this in such a clear voice before everyone if I were to think of him as my brother. As a critical evaluator of his deeds I can place him as someone belonging to the people and in an impartial manner simply give him his dues.

Happily, his total devotion and endeavour is now successful, his childhood wish fulfilled, for Bengal today occupies the first position as far as progress in women's condition is concerned. I would be deviating from the truth if I did not say something here. It is doubtful whether such progress could have been achieved within such a short time without my husband lending his helping hand to my brother. At least it cannot be doubted that he has contributed a great deal to advance this process of progress.

Translated by Subha Chakraborty Dasgupta

From 'সেকেলে কথা', ভারতী, চৈত্র, ১৩২২ বঙ্গাব্দ, মার্চ-এপ্রিল, ১৯১৬।

'Shekele Katha', *Bharati*, Chaitra, 1322 B.S., March-April, 1916.

Notes

This essay was previously published in *Pradip* (Bhadra 1306, B.S., Aug-Sept 1899). The 1322 (1916) version shows that a few changes were made in the first half of the essay. For instance, we cite a paragraph that was a part of the 1306 (1899) edition, but was later deleted:

> I do not know about the state of the general *antahpur* in aristocratic families of Calcutta, but even in those days women's education was not unknown in our *antahpur*. By 'those days' I do not simply mean my childhood days, but the total time frame beginning from the days of my parents to my childhood. My father is now 83 years old, my mother is ten years younger than him. They witnessed the behaviour patterns, rites, culture and education of their parents and moulded themselves accordingly. So it may be said that the above mentioned yesteryears comprise a century.

The second section of the 1306 edition begins with: 'When my mother came to this house as a daughter-in-law.' There are no changes in the later editions after this. Certain statements were added at the beginning in the 1322 edition to make it relevant to the age. Also in the 1306 edition there was a small section at the end, as follows:

> In keeping with the content we now print a copy of a photograph of the respected writer when she was young. Later we intend to present the reader with one of her recent photographs.–Editor, *Pradip*

1 The words of the famous writer Anurupa Devi (1882–1958), who went on to say, 'Many women had written poems and stories before her, but these were looked upon patronizingly. She was the first writer to show up the strength of women's writing and raise women's creations to a position of respect.' In Susie Tharu and K. Lalita, eds, *Women Writing in India, 600 B.C. to the Present* (Delhi: Oxford University Press, 1992), p 235.
2 *Bharati,* a journal with contributions from the most renowned writers of the time, was started in Sravan (July-Aug) 1879 and continued very successfully for 50 years till Aswin (Sept-Oct) 1926, when its last issue

was published. Dwijendranath Tagore was its first editor from 1879 to 1883.

Manilal Ganguly (1888–1929) was a well-known literary figure who edited *Bharati* with Sourindramohan Mukhopadhyay from 1915 to 1923. He has a special place in Bangla literature for his texts such as *Japani Phanush, Jalchhabi, Kalpakatha,* and so on. He was the son-in-law of Abanindranath Tagore, the artist-scholar.

3 The question of women's voting rights became an issue in the late nineteenth century, and the struggle was particularly intense in Great Britain and the United States. In 1897 in Britain, the various suffragist societies united into the National Union of Women's Suffrage societies. Later, a segment of the women suffrage movement became more militant under the leadership of Emmeline Pankhurst and her daughter Christabel, who led violent action and undertook hunger strikes after the defeat of seven suffrage bills in Parliament in the early twentieth century. During World War I the women's suffrage organizations made considerable contributions to war efforts and support for their cause grew. British women won the right to vote in 1918.

4 An illustrated monthly magazine founded in Dec/Jan 1898 (Poush, 1304 B.S.) under the editorship of Ramananda Chattopadhyay. It continued for about eight years.

5 Prince Dwarakanath Tagore (1794–1846), founder of the Jorasanko Tagore family. He knew English and some French. An entrepreneur who imported silk, dealt in indigo, and bought coal mines, he also handled shipping, established sugar mills and added to the estates he had inherited. He established the Union Bank in 1829, becoming its chief director in 1831. In 1842 he travelled to England on business and died there in 1846, and was buried in the grounds of Kensal Green Church.

6 The Vaishnava sect constitutes one of the most important religious sects in Bengal, which also gave women an important place within it. Travelling as mendicants, the Vaishnavas were treated with a great deal of respect in upper class households. Both male and female Vaishnavas acted as preachers and singers. The female Vaishnavi had more mobility than women in upper class households and acquired some literacy as part of her religious pursuit.

7 Published in 1856, these two books laid the foundation of spelling and grammar in Bangla. Iswarchandra Vidyasagar (1820–1891), was the author.

8 Dwijendranath Tagore's *Tattvavidya*, a physical and metaphysical discourse, was published in four vols:

1st vol : *Gyankanda* (8 Agrahayan 1788 Saka/1866)
2nd vol : *Bhogkanda* (18 October 1867)
3rd vol : *Karmakanda* (23 February 1868)
4th vol : *Sadhan Prakaran* (10 May 1869)

9 Ramnarayan Tarkaratna (1822–86) wrote the first structured play in Bangla and came to be known as 'Natukey Ramnarayan'. His plays were staged in the houses of the rich. A student of Sanskrit College, he taught at Hindu Metropolitan College. He won awards for his books *Patibratopakhyan* and *Kulinkulsarbasya*. Among his important plays and *prahasans* are *Ratnabali, Benisanhar, Nabanatak* and *Jemon Karma Temni Phal*.

10 *Hutom Pyanchar Naksha* (Part I, 1862; Parts I and II, 1864) by Kaliprasanna Sinha (1840–1870) provides a very clear contemporary sketch of private and public life of Calcutta. Written in colloquial prose it satirizes the society of this time.

 Pyarichand Mitra (1814–1883), a disciple of Derozio, was a student of Hindu College who knew English and Persian equally well. He was a member of the Senate of Calcutta University, and one of the chief organizers and secretary of Bethune Society and British India Society. He regularly wrote for the *Englishman, Calcutta Review, Hindu Patriot, Indian Field* and other journals. He was the joint editor with Radhanath Sikdar of *Masik Patrika*, a journal which tried to improve the condition of women and where he serially published his best novel, *Alaler Gharer Dulal*. His use of colloquial Bangla in the text opened up new possibilities of language usage and the form came to be known as *Alali Bhasha*. Some of his other important writings are *Abhedi, Jatkinchit, Mad Khaoa Boro Dai Jat Thakar Ki Upai, Krishipath*.

11 Bharatchandra Roy, Raygunakar (1717–1760) was the the court poet of Maharaj Krishnachandra at whose request he composed *Annadamangal* and received the title of Raygunakar. He is also the author of *Vidyasundar* and *Rasamanjari*. As the first metropolitan poet of Bangla literature, he brought new dimensions to it: graceful language, dexterous rhythms and a fine portrayal of characters.

12 Madanmohan Tarkalankar (1817–1858) was a student of Sanskrit College and a contemporary of Iswarchandra Vidyasagar. He was given the title of 'Tarkalankar' for his scholarly abilities. *Basabdatta* was published in 1836. He taught at Fort William College and Krishnanagar

College. In 1855 he was promoted to the post of Deputy Magistrate. He sent his two daughters Bhubanmala and Kundamala to Bethune School when it was established in 1849.
13 Girindranath Tagore (1820–1854) was the second brother of Debendranath Tagore and the author's uncle. Satyendranath writes in *Amar Balyakatha* (1915), 'Mejokaka was a large-hearted, pleasure loving gentleman of discerning taste . . . He had a deep love for both the arts and the sciences. He would often entertain us and himself with scientific experiments . . . As in science, Mejokaka was also well-versed in literature . . . He wrote a play named *Babubilas* which was also once enacted . . . Mejokaka was talented in every sphere. Debendranath's autobiography mentions his skills regarding material concerns.' Gaganendranath and Abanindranath are two of his famous grandsons.
14 Maharshi Debendranath Tagore (1817–1905), the son of Prince Dwarakanath Tagore, received his early education in the Anglo-Hindu School established by Rammohan Roy and then at Hindu College. Religious questions became very important to him after the death of his grandmother and in order to discuss religious issues he established the Tattaranjini Sabha in 1839, which later became the famous Tattvabodhini Sabha. In 1842 it became linked with the Brahmo Samaj. He was initiated into the Brahmo religion in 1843. In 1859 he established Brahmavidyalay and in 1850 became its high priest. In 1861 it was with his financial assistance that *Indian Mirror* was published. The Brahmo Samaj split up in 1866 with differences of opinion on the part of Keshabchandra Sen, and Debendranath's Samaj was renamed Adi Brahmo Samaj. Debendranath was given the title of 'Maharshi' by Brahmos in 1869.
15 This school for girls in Calcutta was founded by John Elliot Drinkwater Bethune with the help of local people on 7 May 1849. It was a pioneering effort in the cause of women's education and Bethune willed his entire property to the school. After his death it came to be known as Bethune School and then Bethune Collegiate School. The history of Bethune School and College is intimately associated with the history of women's education in Bengal. Many young women who made notable contributions to education and society were its graduates, including Kadambini Basu (later Ganguly) who was the first woman to sit for the entrance examination of Calcutta University in 1878. Chandramukhi Bose, a graduate of the college that was founded in 1879, became the first woman to obtain an M.A. from

the University of Calcutta (see also 16, Sarala Devi, 'My Life Changes Track', n17, this volume).

16 Keshabchandra Sen (1838–1884) was educated at Hindu College (1848–1858) and at Hindu Metropolitan College. He joined the Brahmo Samaj in 1857, becoming very close to Maharshi Debendranath, rising fast to become one of its leaders, achieving fame as a patriot and an orator. He attracted students by establishing Brahmovidyalay in 1859. From 1861 he began to publish *Indian Mirror* and the *Sunday Mirror*. Later he published *Brahmodharmer Anusthan* in order to emphasize the differences between the Hindus and the Brahmos, which eventually caused a split between the followers of Debendranath and Keshabchandra, and in 1866 the latter established the Bharatbarshiya Brahma Samaj and in 1869 the Bharatiya Brahmamandir. In 1871 he also established the Native Ladies' Normal and Adult School for the education of girls, which later became an institute of higher education known as the Victoria Institution. In 1878 he got his daughter Suniti married at an age below the one accepted by the Brahmos, causing a further split. *Jeebanved, Nabasamhita* and *Jog* are some of his well-known books.

17 Satyendranath Tagore (1842–1923), the second son of Maharshi Debendranath, and the author's second eldest brother, became famous as the first Indian ICS and went to work in Bombay. He was appointed collector and magistrate at Ahmedabad in 1865. He was in favour of women's education and freedom along with all other schemes to improve the condition of women. He encouraged his wife, Jnanadanandini, to take up similar work free from the shackles of tradition and to propagate new norms of behaviour. He retired from government service in 1916. His book *Amar Balyakatha o Amar Bombai Prabash* is one of the best of the genre in Bangla literature.

18 Ayodhyanath Pakrashi (?-1873), Sanskrit scholar and chief translator in the group that translated Kaliprasanna Sinha's *Mahabharata*. Appointed Adhyaksha of the Brahmo Samaj, he edited *Tattvabodhini Patrika* from 1865–1867 and from 1869–1873. *Brahmovidyalay* (1870) is one of his important books.

19 Hemendranath Tagore (1845–1884) was the third son of Maharshi Debendranath, and the author's brother, who tried diligently to bring in education to the antahpur. Jnanadanandini wrote, 'It seemed that our brother-in law Hemendanath Tagore took up the task of teaching us with deliberation. We covered our heads and sat before him and we were startled when he scolded us. I learnt whatever Bangla I know from Sejothakurpo [Hemendranath].'

20 Satyendranath said, 'I supported women's independence from childhood
   . . .My favourite text was John Stuart Mill's *Subjection of Women;* and
   having read the text, I brought out a pamphlet entitled "Women's
   Independence".' *Amar Balyakatha,* p.4. *Sahitya-Sadhak-Charitmala,*
   vol.6 (Calcutta: Bangiya Sahitya Parishad, Kartik 1378, Oct–Nov 1971
   ed).
21 Sarada Devi (1826?–1875) was married to Debendranath Tagore in
   1834 when she was probably eight years old.. She spent the first years
   of her life with Hindu rites and rituals. Later when Debendranath
   turned to Brahmodharma, Hindu rites and rituals were gradually done
   away with to her great distress. Her life was spent in conflict between
   these two religious worlds.
22 Janakinath Ghosal (1840–1913) was educated at Krishnanagar
   Collegiate School. He lost faith in the caste system and discarded his
   sacred thread. His father disowned him on hearing the news. He then
   took up various projects for the uplift of society. He married the
   author who was the fourth daughter of Maharshi Debendranath. Later
   he went to England to study law. He was the Municipal Commissioner
   for Calcutta for quite some time. He joined the Theosophical Society
   when Madam Blavatsky visited India.
23 Hiranmoyee Devi (1868–1925) was the eldest daughter of the author.
   She was educated at Bethune School. She wrote for the periodicals
   Sakha, Balak, Bharati, and *Bharati o Balak.* In 1906 she established
   'Bidhoba Shilpasram', a place where widows could work. Many of
   her fervent patriotic articles during the freedom movement were
   published in *Bharati.* See 12, 'Proposal: An Arts Association/A Women's
   Art Association', this volume.
24 The mother of eleven children, Neepomoyee could sing, draw, read
   books in different languages and cook both Indian and Western food.
   She is also said to have excelled in drawing portraits of members of
   the family.
       Bisnuchandra Chakraborty (1804–1900) was born in Kayatpara,
   Nadia. He learnt dhrupad from Hannu Khan and Dilawar Khan and
   khayal from Miyan Miran. He was appointed singer in the Brahmo
   Mandir established by Raja Rammohan in 1828. He remained in the
   Brahmo Samaj for a long time as singer, composer and as *sangeetacharya,*
   composing the tunes of the songs of the first six volumes of the
   twelve-volume *Brahmosangeet.* He was the *sangeetacharya* of the Tagore
   family. He also composed the tune for Satyendranath Tagore's famous
   song 'Mile sabe bharat-santan' on the occasion of the Hindu Mela.

He composed the songs of *Nabanatak* (1867) enacted in the family theatre at Jorasanko and provided the music for *Neeldarpan* (7 December 1872) that was being staged for the first time in the public theatre.

25 Pratibha Devi (1865–1922) was the eldest daughter of Hemendranath Tagore and the author's niece She studied at home under the guidance of her father and showed great talent for music even as a teenager. Her musical notations were published in *Bharati* and *Bharati o Balak*. She married barrister Asutosh Chaudhuri, well-known for his social activities. She established Sangeet Sangha to teach music. She also edited a periodical named *Ananda Sangeet Patrika* with Indira Devi Chaudhurani, her uncle Satyendranath Tagore's daughter..

16 Sarala Devi Chaudhurani

Sarala Devi Chaudhurani (1872–1945) was the daughter of Janakinath Ghosal and Swarnakumari Devi and was thus born into a home of privilege, intellectual achievements, where it was accepted that women would be educated and emancipated. She came first among the women candidates for the B.A. Hons in 1890 and received the Padmavati medal. She taught at the Maharani School at Mysore, leaving her home in Calcutta to take up that task with confidence and self-reliance. With characteristic enthusiasm and determination she threw herself into the Swadeshi movement and launched the Pratapaditya Utsav and the Veerashtami Brata to propagate nationalist sentiments, also founding Lakshmir Bhandar to encourage the use of indigenous goods. She edited Bharati, *and later in Lahore with her husband, Pandit Rambhuj Dutt Chaudhuri, ran the Urdu paper* Hindustan, *of which she brought out an English version. She was proficient in music and wrote a number of patriotic songs. Among her books are* Jeebaner Jharapata: Bangalir Pitridhan; Nababarsher Swapna; Bharat Stree Mahamandal; *and* Shata Gan.

My Life Changes Track

As I have mentioned elsewhere, following my early attempts at writing, published in *Balak*,[1] it was an unsigned comic piece, 'Premik Sabha' in *Bharati*,[2] that led to my waking up one morning and finding myself famous, like Byron. A lot of praise showered down from all sides, and unexpectedly, without revealing the secret to anybody else, Robimama [Rabindranath Tagore] sent his congratulations: 'The piece has been correctly assessed because you did not put your name to it. This is no amateur's writing; it comes from the pen of a fully mature author. I would not have felt embarrassed even if people had mistaken it for my own writing.'[3]

Such great praise struck me speechless in my humble joy. But the publication of this piece also created a minor predicament for me. Some people, suspecting that the cap fitted them, looked bemused, others, less patient, began to direct irate glances at me. However, this storm in a teacup soon subsided; *'Premik Sabha'* did not get dissolved like *Chirakumar Sabha,* but continued intact.[4]

Now my pen ran on without let. Articles on classical Sanskrit literature were coming out. The first one was on Rati's lamentation from *Kumarasambhavam.*[5]

Hiren Dutta sent a message applauding the genuine novelty in this piece.[6] Much later, two or three years before his death, once when I was reading out my 'Niler Uposh' to him, he praised its content and style and remarked, 'Why don't you put all your pieces together in the form of a book? You are depriving the literary world of Bengal. Your 'Rati-Bilap' created a sensation. You have not as yet put all those things together in a single publication. You might even do it now.'

Malabika-Agnimitra was the next in the series.[7] I have noted earlier that I sent this one to Bankimbabu for his perusal.[8] I have also narrated before how the invaluable letter I received from him on this piece got destroyed in the political conflagration in Punjab. Robimama's letter on *Malabika-Agnimitra* was similarly lost. Not only this one, but others received from him since my childhood—about fifty in number—have been also swallowed up by Time, the great devourer.

The next to appear was *Malati-Madhava.*[9] All these texts had been part of my syllabus at the F.A. (First Arts) and the B.A. level. I had started on *Mrichchakatikam,* but that was never completed.[10] At one point, I even made an effort to publish these articles together as a book with the title *'Kabi Mandir'.* Dinesh Sen was entrusted with the work, since at that time I was already about to depart for Lahore.[11] After two or three formes had been printed, however, Dinesh babu lost interest. I was not even able to retrieve the printed parts, although I had paid the press its dues in full in advance. The lesson learnt from this was that for a non-resident to attempt to bring out a book through someone else is but to burn good money. Later, after returning to Bengal, whenever I took the initiative to publish it again, the fearsome shadow of the World War intervened, and everybody discouraged me because paper had become so costly.

In the meantime, I went to Solapur with my mother to visit Mejomama [Satyendranath Tagore] for a few months.[12] At Dussera, that is, the celebrations on the final day of Durga Puja, at the Marathi Club, the Gaekwad of Baroda made an appearance. The monarch had excellent manners, and his courtesy to my mother and me charmed us. But what impressed me most were the celebrations we witnessed that day. Lathi and sword play, along with various gymnastic feats, predominated; there were also heroic and inspiring speeches. It struck a completely different chord from our own traditions of the dancing of *baijis*, music and drinking bouts.

Then at Poona we also attended a fancy dress ball for the civilians of Bombay Presidency. In a room full of Europeans, there were only three Indians—Mejomama, my mother and me. I recall that my mother was dressed up as a sanyasini and I was the Goddess Saraswati. This sanyasini's garb suited my mother very well, and for the Spring festival [in Calcutta], too, she played the role of the sanyasini to Natunmami's neglected heroine—as far as I remember, the latter succeeded in regaining the favour of her beloved through the grace of the sanyasini.[13] The occasion of the Poona visit that time was the Civil Service Ball. But it failed to have any lasting impact on my mind; the effect vanished like drops of water on a lotus leaf. It only recalled to my mind Loken's experience on the day when he had perceived an irreconcilable breach between himself and the Englishman.[14] A more lasting emotion agitated my mind once when I happened to have a frontal view of a Peshwa pillar while passing through Sanicharpet in the town of Poona. This was followed by an article in *Bharati*: 'The Bengali and the Marathi'.[15] The games held on Dussera and the sight of the Peshwa pillar as a commemoration of heroism sowed in my mind the idea of the 'Veerashtami' festival. God, the Holder of the Threads of all happenings in this world, put in my hands at that time a clue to a possible regeneration of the national character of the Bengalis through working a change in the character of their national festivals.

Today in every house, in every school, at every meeting, girls dancing is a common sight. In those days, even taking a couple of rhythmic steps on stage was frowned upon. Once, with a lot of trepidation, I taught some young girls a bare semblance of rhythmic movements while Rabindranath's lyric: 'Come dear friends, let us dance together holding hands and singing songs' was being presented. However, there was another episode signifying even greater boldness on my part. I had entered Bethune School when I was seven and a half.[16] Almost ten years later, at the age of 17, I graduated from Bethune College. But my ties with the school continued. Every year, when the prize distribution ceremony was being held, the superintendent Miss Chandramukhi Bose and her successor, Kumudini Khastagir, would invite me to prepare the girls for a musical programme to be presented by them.[17] One of the songs I taught them was composed by me:

> 'We pay our homage to you, Mother India,
> Wearing knowledge on your head as a diadem,
> How the jewels of glory
> Achieved by your blessed son through his penance
> Shine on your garland.'[18]

This had been composed on the occasion when Natunmama[19] presented Jagadish Bose[20] with a citation on behalf of his Sangeet Samaj. Not many were familiar with the song. While this song was being rehearsed by the students of Bethune School, Bipin Pal came out with a remark about this song in his paper.[21] He wrote that at his home the girls were rehearsing a song, the words had wafted to his ears. All the patriotic songs composed so far had a note of despair about them, nostalgia for the past giving them a mournful character. He was astonished to observe that this particular song was different in spirit; it confronted the present with courage and enthusiasm and looked to the future with joyous confidence.

However, on prize day, when the song was sung in front of Sir Gurudas Banerjee, a member of the School Committee, he showed signs of embarrassment.[22] The next day Sir Gurudas called on Chandramukhi Bose and told her that the song should not have been sung at the school, since it ended with the following lines :

'Knowledge is here, prosperity will come
Along with power and glory,
Armed with weapons, O Mother,
Will you make amends for your degraded state?'[23]

In our days, boys and girls never studied together in the same institution. After I joined the F.A. class, I developed a strong desire to study science as one of my subjects even as Sudhidada [Sudhindranath Tagore] and others were doing.[24] No such opportunity was available at Bethune College. My repeated appeals to the Education Department bore no fruit. Ultimately arrangements were made for me to join the evening lectures at the Science Association founded by Dr. Mahendralal Sarkar,[25] who was a friend of Babamashai [father].[26] The lecture hall was filled with male students coming from the F.A. classes of different colleges. I was the only girl student. Before the lecture started, I would accompany Dr. Sarkar and Father Lafont to their room and sit there.[27] Sudhidada and my own elder brother would also be with me. When the time came, the lecturer would proceed towards the hall with me tagging along, the two elder brothers flanking me on either side. The boys would murmur 'bodyguards' as we passed them. There would be rows of benches for the students, but in the front row three chairs would be kept for us.

This is how I took my lessons in physics. I might have taken botany at Bethune, since this required no apparatus. But I was determined that I would study physics to remain on par with the boys in my family. Apart from these lectures, I also got some assistance from Jogesh babu, the second brother of Ashu babu.[28] This was before his visit to Europe, he was probably teaching science at Metropolitan College at the time. Thus my resolve was fulfilled, and I gained entry to physical science, passed the test, and even got a silver medal from the Science Association. Since that time, I also became closely acquainted with Father Lafont. He was not just a teacher at St. Xavier's College, but appeared at entertainments and at social occasions like evening parties and dinners, and was full of cheerful conversation and friendliness.

When I was studying for my B.A., two Christian girls from Miss Thoburne's School at Lucknow joined my class. One was a Bengali, Sharat Chakraborty, and the other was a Hindustani, her name was Edith Rafael. Sharat was the stereotype of the 'native' Christian girl—full of missionary zeal. From her own words I learnt that she was an adept at spiriting away Hindu girls from their homes to convert them to Christianity, at concealing them and keeping their relatives in the dark. Ethel was of a different nature; she too was a firm believer in Christianity, but incapable of deception or duality. She was not beautiful, but her eyes had a certain wistfulness that immediately attracted people to her. Robimama also made the same observation when he happened to see her at our house one day.

After she came to Bethune College and became my classmate, Ethel went through a period of mental turmoil. At that time, in Punjab and in western India, when the missionaries converted someone to Christianity, it was usual for them to make the convert relinquish the Indian name and title and adopt an English one. That is how Ethel was Miss Rafael. But her family was of Rajput lineage, and had the indigenous title 'Singh'. Through her association with us, she imbibed strong nationalist sentiments. When she went to Lucknow during the summer vacation, she gave up 'Ethel Rafael' and adopted the name 'Leela Singh' through a notification to the magistrate. Probably in the calendar of Calcutta University, too, she appeared as 'Leela Singh'. It was as 'Leela Singh' and clad in a sari, rather than in a frock, that she was sent to the USA from Thoburne College as a representative of Christian women in India. Patriotism fully blossomed in her. These days, the policy of the missionaries is to retain the indigenous name of the convert. The other practice, in fact, led to a big uproar in Lahore. Some people were using the talisman of the English name given to them by the missionaries to receive emoluments on the same scale as the Europeans.

When the government came to know of this, it forced them to add an indigenous surname to the English name, so that they could be identified as 'natives' and paid their salary on a lower scale. Leela Singh on the other hand, voluntarily went back to her family name and set an example of self-respect.

After graduation, for two or three years, I was fully occupied in running *Bharati*. The thought of marriage was furthest from my mind; it was as if 'my mind and soul was dedicated to myself'.[29] I began to prepare for an M.A. in Sanskrit at home. When Mahesh Nyayaratna learnt about this, he came out with a threat: Let us see how she manages to get an M.A. in Sanskrit without getting herself registered at Sanskrit College. This increased the determination of my tutor, Pandit Sitalchandra Vedantabagish, to see me through my M.A. He started teaching me *Samkhya Karika*. One or two of the questions I asked him pleased him so much that he said that only one other student had plied him with such questions, that was Hiren Dutta, a veritable jewel of a student.

However, in spite of the challenge thrown by Mahesh Nyayaratna, I did not finally complete my M.A. My mind was in a great turmoil. I longed to rush out of the cage that was my home, to go out on a tryst with the unknown, to exercise the right to earn my own living like my brothers. I began to pester my parents until Babamashai in exasperation gave his consent. It remained to inform Karta Dadamashai [Debendranath Tagore] and to get him to agree.[30] He had never gone against the independent wishes and ways even of his own children in the new era. It was obvious that he would not object where the grandchildren were concerned. When Mejomama took Mejomami [Jnandanandini Devi][31] along with him to England, and subsequently when after returning from England, she accompanied him to the party at the Governor's house, Karta Dadamoshai did not raise any objections. However, Jatindramohan Tagore[32] and others were so embarrassed to see a daughter-in-law of the family in a public place, that they avoided the couple, and the old servants of the family shed tears to see Mejomami walking up to the main gate to get into the car. In those days, my mother and my aunts would be carried in the palanquin right from the inner quarters to the embankment of the Ganges, and then be dipped into the water inside the closed palanquins if they wanted to have a bath in the Ganges [see 15, 'Words from Times Past']. Even if they wanted to visit Gagandada's family [Gagendranath Tagore],[33] they would make their way there in the palanquin. When such women broke all those time-honoured conventions to chart the course along which Mejomama's wishes were taking them, Karta Dadamashai had never objected, so why should he object in my case? But still he would have to be informed, I would have to seek his blessings. When he was told that I wanted to leave, he did not oppose me. But he sent a message through Boromashima [Saudamini Devi].[34] If Sarala takes a vow never to get married, then before she leaves, I can wed her to the sword.

The proposal was romantic enough, but I pondered over it and asked the depths of my own being: Was I prepared to take a vow that I would never get married? In the days when Theosophy had great prevalence, a 'Mataji' from Benares would often visit our house. My mother would say: we shall not give Sarala in marriage; like Mataji, she would dedicate her life to her country's welfare. Like a blade of grass, the young mind gets carried away along the current on which her parents place it. In this case, my mind had been drawn in the direction of not marrying and was standing balanced on its verge. Mother changed her mind later and was very keen to get me married. But I remained out of reach— rejecting all names that she proposed. But when Karta Dadamashai required me to take a vow abjuring marriage, my mind rose in rebellion. I tested myself and found that I was not at all prepared to accept perpetual spinsterhood through a vow. No woman could make this her ultimate goal. I was still content to go along with my own will, but a day might come when I would make another's will mine own; my mind could not brook the thought of undoing that possibility once and for all with my own hands.

When Babamashai granted me his consent, he did so with the secret hope that I would not find any place to go to. Where would there be a suitable job waiting for me? There was, however, such a job. When I had gone on a tour of Mysore with Sarala Ray[35] and others, I had not met the Maharaja—he had been away in Ootacamund. The Dewan and other high officials there had formed a very high opinion of me as I was the saintly Debendranath's granddaughter. I sent a telegram to Narasingh Ayengar Darbar Bakshi, who was the uncle of Dr. Ramaswami. Ayengar was very influential in the state, being the Maharaja's favourite and was the founder and all-in-all of Maharani Girls' School. The telegram ran: *Want to serve the School. Wire if opening available.* Within two days, came the reply: *Always opening for you. Start as soon as you like.* Later Ayengar told me that he was overjoyed when he got my telegram and went and told the Maharaja: A daughter of an A1 family wishes to join our school on her own. This is a unique opportunity.

Mejomama was in Satara at the time. Satara was on the way to Mysore via Bombay. Mother went with me up to Satara. Then Mejomama accompanied me from Satara to Mysore as my guardian. He had no qualms in his mind about women taking up jobs. He was in favour of social reform at all levels. He did not consider it an indignity for the family that the Maharshi's granddaughter was going to take up a job. He reached me to Mysore and returned after being satisfied that all necessary conveniences were there.

Kumudini Khastagir was then assistant superintendent in the same school. It so happened that at that time it became necessary for her to leave her job and come to Calcutta. So neither the Dewan nor the Darbar Bakshi needed to create a separate post for me. Kumudini's post became available for me at once. The authorities also intended to raise me to the post of Lady Superintendent as soon as the English lady who was in that post, and was universally unpopular, completed her year of contract with the school. I only had to wait for the interim period to be over.

Thus I landed upon a new course, separated from all relatives and friends. My life took a new turn.

Translated by Malini Bhattacharya

From 'জীবনের মোড়ফেরা', চতুর্দশ অধ্যায়, জীবনের ঝরাপাতা,
কলকাতা: সাহিত্য সংসদ, ফাল্গুন, ১৮৭৯ শকাব্দ, ফেব্রুয়ারী-মার্চ, ১৯৫৭।

'Jeeboner Mor Phera', in *Jeeboner Jhorapata*, Chapter 14, Calcutta: Sahitya Samsad, Phalgun, 1879 Saka, Feb-March, 1957.

Notes

1 This illustrated monthly magazine was first published in Baisakh, 1292 B.S. (mid-April–mid-May1885), and edited by Jnanadanandini Devi, the wife of Satyendranath Tagore, for a year. It was meant for older boys and girls. After a year it was merged with *Bharati*. See also 15, Swarnakumari Devi, 'Words from Times Past', n22.
2 This piece was published anonymously in *Bharati o Balak* in Ashar, 1298 B.S. (June-July 1891).
3 The author's maternal uncle, Rabindranath Tagore. He was the youngest brother of Swarnakumari Devi, the author's mother.
4 Written by Rabindranath Tagore it was first published in *Bharati*, 1307–08 B.S. (1901–1902) serially. In 1314 B.S. (1907), the text was published as *Prajapatir Nirbandhya*. After considerable texual changes and alterations the book was finally published as a play, *Chirakumar Sabha*, in 1332 B.S. (1925).
5 Epic poem by Kalidasa on the birth of the God Kartikeya. The episode of Rati's lament, constituting one of the most lyrical passages in the poem, comes when her consort, Madana, the love god, is burnt to ashes by the fire from Shiva's eyes.
6 Hirendranath Dutta (1868–1942), eminent scholar, philosopher, and politician, who was among the Moderates in Congress, and worked very closely with Annie Besant from 1894–1920. He founded the Hindu Mahasabha with Madan Mohan Malviya.
7 Five-act play written by Kalidasa celebrating the love-affair between Malavika and King Agnimitra.
8 Bankimchandra Chattopadhyay (1838–1894), most eminent of the writers of the modern Bangla novel; as an essayist, thinker and editor, he exercised an enormous influence on Bengali social and intellectual life.
9 Play in ten acts by Bhababhuti, one of the most famous dramatists after Kalidasa. It is conjectured that he lived ca A.D. eighth century.
10 *Mrichchakatikam* was written between A.D. third and fifth centuries, supposedly by King Sudraka, and gives valuable insights into contemporary social and political life.
11 Dineshchandra Sen (1866–1939) worked extensively to recover lost folk traditions and folklore of Bengal; a pioneer in the study of the history of Bengali literature, he was Reader and Ramtanu Lahiri Research Fellow, Department of Bengali, University of Calcutta.

12 The author's second eldest maternal uncle, Satyendranath Tagore (1842–1923), who was the first Indian member of the Indian Civil Service and held many high administrative posts during his career. He had very progressive ideas about the social status of women and introduced many radical changes within the family. See also 15, Swarnakumari Devi, 'Words from Times Past', this volume.

13 Kadambari Devi (1859–1885), the wife of Jyotirindranath Tagore, the author's matenal uncle's wife. Married in 1868 to Jyotirindranath Tagore, the fifth son of Debendranath Tagore, she was interested in literature and theatre and wielded enormous influence on Rabindranath Tagore, her youngest brother-in-law. Her sudden suicide in April 1885 was a shock that haunted Rabindranath all his life.

14 Lokendranath Palit (1865–1915) joined the Indian Civil Service (ICS) in 1886 and was appointed to many administrative posts in Bengal and Bihar. He was a patron of the National Council of Education, Bengal, established in 1906, and was a friend of Rabindranath Tagore with whom he engaged in many literary debates.

15 'Bangali o Marhatti', *Bharati o Balak,* Sravan 1299 B.S. (July-Aug 1892).

16 'Native Female School' founded by John Elliot Drinkwater Bethune (1801–1851) in Calcutta in 1849 for promoting public education for girls in Bengal. See also 15, Swarnakurmari Devi, "Words from Times Past', n14.

17 Chandramukhi Bose (1860–1944) was born in a Bengali Christian family and she became the first woman to receive an M.A. degree from the University of Calcutta in 1884. She became the first Principal of Bethune College when it became a separate institution. Kumudini Khastagiri (1865–?) graduated from Bethune College and taught at Bethune School and subsequently at Bethune College, becoming its Principal in 1902.

18 নমো নমো ভারত জননি . . .
বিদ্যামুকুটধারিণী!
বরপুত্রের তপ-অর্জিত,
গৌরব মণিমালিনী!

19 Jyotirindranath Tagore (1849–1925), the author's maternal uncle who was the fifth son of Debendranath Tagore, was extremely talented, composed songs, wrote and produced plays, translated from French and Marathi, and was the founder of Bharat Sangeet Samaj. He was also one of the pioneers in inculcating patriotism through Sanjibani Sabha and initiated many indigenous industrial and business enterprises, most of which however failed.

My Life Changes Track   171

20 Jagadish Chandra Bose (1858–1937) was a renowned physicist and botanist. He gave up his job in Presidency College to protest against the disparity in remuneration between British and Indian teachers. For his work in the area of electromagnetic waves he received a D.Sc. from London University in 1896. Subsequently he extended his area of research to plant organisms and made important contributions in understanding plant reactions to electromagnetic currents. He founded Basu Vijnan Mandir in 1917, became the president of the Indian Science Congress in 1927 and later the president of Bangiya Sahitya Parishad. Apart from his scientific books in English he was a pioneer in writing on popular science in Bangla.

21 Bipin Chandra Pal (1858–1932), eminent Congress leader and a great orator who took part in the Swadeshi movement that followed the Partition of Bengal (1905), working closely with Surendranath Banerjea. He was the first editor of the English daily *Vande Mataram* (1906). A follower of Lala Lajpat Rai and Balgangadhar Tilak, he retired from active politics in 1921 after differences with Mahatma Gandhi.

22 Sir Gurudas Banerjee (1844–1918) had a brilliant career as a student and taught at Berhampore College. From 1872 he practised as lawyer in Calcutta High Court and became a judge in 1888. He was also involved with education policy and was a member of the syndicate of the University of Calcutta and associated with the foundation of Jadavpur University.

23 এসেছে বিদ্যা, আসিবে ঋদ্ধি / শৌর্যবীর্যশালিনী / অপমানক্ষত জুড়াইবি মাতঃ / খর্পরকরবালিনি!

24 Sudhindranath Tagore (1869–1929), the author's cousin, and son of Dwijendranath Tagore, her mother's eldest brother. He wrote in a number of magazines and periodicals and edited *Sadhana* for a few years.

25 Dr. Mahendralal Sarkar (1833–1904) received the degree of I.M.S. from Calcutta Medical College in 1861 and became M.D. in 1863. He published the *Calcutta Journal of Medicine* in 1867 and founded the Indian Association for the Cultivation of Science in 1876 to provide opportunity for indigenous scientific research.

26 Janakinath Ghosal (1840–1913), the author's father, whom she addressed with respect as Babamashai. See also 15, Swarnakumari Devi, 'Words from Time Past', n21, this volume.

27 Fr. Lafont, Belgian missionary who joined the Society of Jesuits in 1854, and was sent to Calcutta in 1865. He became lecturer in experimental science and subsequently the Rector of St. Xavier's College

in 1871. Jagadish Chandra Bose was one of his students (see n20). He was the first to be awarded Doctor of Science *(Honoris Causa)* by the University of Calcutta in 1908.

28 Sir Ashutosh Chaudhuri (1860–1924), barrister in the Calcutta High Court, adopted Brahmoism after marrying Pratibha Devi, the granddaughter of Debendranath Tagore (see n30). An enthusiastic supporter of the Swadeshi movement, he took a leading role in the establishment of the National Council of Education, Bengal, pioneered the foundation of Bengal Technical College and Bangalakshmi Cotton Mill and was the founder secretary of the Bengal Landholders' Association. Relations between his family and the Tagore family were very close. He was also an author of literary and political articles.

29 Here she quotes a line from Rabindranath Tagore's early operatic work Mayar Khela, which had been performed by Sakhi Samity: 'আপনার মন আপনার প্রাণ আপনারে সঁপিয়াছি।'

30 Debendranath Tagore (1817–1905), the author's maternal grandfather and one of the founders of Adi Brahmo Samaj, whose influence as a religious leader was widespread in mid-nineteenth century Bengal. He was interested in women's education and initiated and supported many social reforms. See also 15, Swarnakumari Devi, 'Words from Times Past', this volume.

31 The author's aunt by marriage, Jnanadanandini Devi (1852–1941), married to Satyendranath Tagore, the second son of Debendranath Tagore in 1857. Defying the social norms of the time Satyendranath (see also 15, Swarnakumari Devi, 'Words from Times Past', this volume) took pains to educate her. She edited *Balak* for a year, also wrote children's books and an autobiography. Adopting the style of Parsee women she initiated a new way of wearing the sari for Bengali women who were beginning to come out of seclusion (see also 8, Hemantakumari Chaudhuri, 'Women's Dress', this volume). She travelled with her children to England without any male escort and remained there for their schooling. She participated in many of the family plays produced by Jyotirindranath in the Tagore household.

32 Jatindramohan Tagore (1831–1908), son of the famous landowning family of Pathuriaghata, a Hindu branch of the Tagore family of Jorasanko.. He was the secretary and then the president of the British Indian Association and a patron of music and of the theatre.

33 Gaganendranath Tagore (1866–1938): Great nephew of Debendranath and one of the most talented members of the larger Jorasanko family, he was a painter and an artist in his own right and also a gifted

cartoonist; a great experimentor in art form who organized the Indian Society for Oriental Arts in 1907. He also founded Bengal Home Industries Association in 1916 for the promotion of indigenous handicrafts.

34 The author's eldest maternal aunt, Saudamini Devi (1847–1920), was the eldest daughter of Debendranath. In 1851 she was sent to Bethune School by her father. She was married to Saradaprasad Ganguly and after the death of her mother, Sarada Devi, ran the household.

35 Sarala Ray (1861–1946) was the eldest daughter of Durgamohan Das, well-known social reformer of the Brahmo Samaj. She studied in Hindu Mahila Vidyalaya and Banga Mahila Vidyalaya. She dedicated her life to the cause of women's education. She was the first woman secretary of Brahmo Girls' School. She also founded Nari Siksha Mandir in Dhaka and Gokhale Memorial School and College in Calcutta. Her role as an educationist was recognized by the University of Calcutta when she was made the first woman member of the Senate.

Index

Adi Brahmo Samaj, 7, 16–20, 144–47.
  See also Roy, Rammohan; Sen, Keshabchandra; Tagore, Debendranath
Antahpur, 92
antahpur, inner quarters, 7, 49, 51, 122, 147, 149
  dress, 94, 95, 148. *See also* dress
  and education, 141–46, 150–51. *See also* education
  as Kalabhavans, 123–24

Balak, 121, 160, 169n1, 172n31.
  See also Devi, Jnanadanandini; Chaudhurani, Sarala Devi
Bamabodhina Patrika, x, 4
Banerjee, Sir Gurdas, 103n3, 164, 177n22
Bangadarshan, 12, 59, 161
Bangiya Sahitya Parishad, 104
banshajas. *See* kulin/Kuliniam
Battala literature, 48, 53n9, 145
beauty, 29, 57, 74, 78–79, 96–97, 105, 121
Bethune College, 162–66. *See also* Chaudhurani, Sarala Devi
Bethune School, 4, 92, 146, 156n15, 163. *See also* Chaudhurani, Sarala Devi
Bharati, 11, 141, 153n2, 160
Bharati o Balak, 59, 81. *See also* Devi, Swarnakumari
Bose, Chandramukhi, 163, 164, 170n17. *See also* Bethune College

Brahmoism, 18, 19, 20, 146–47.
  See also Adi Brahmo Samaj; Roy, Rammohan
bratas, 124–27, 129
British as colonizers, 10–11, 14, 69, 75, 88, 89, 93, 95, 96. *See also* Curzon; Swadeshi

caste, 1, 13, 19, 20, 24, 39, 65, 85.
  See also kulins/Kulinism
  baidya, 29, 53n1, n6
  brahmin, 7, 30, 36–40
  kayastha, 30, 53n3
Chattopadhyay, Bankimchandra, 12, 161, 169n8
child marriage, 23, 29, 40–44, 55, 146.
  See also kulin/Kulinism
Chaudhurani, Sarala Devi, 9, 119n1, 160–64, 168. *See also* discourse
Chaudhuri, Akshay Chandra, 11
Christians/Christianity, ix, 4, 165–66, 172n27
class, 1–3, 6–7, 10–12, 16, 29, 65, 122
Curzon, George Nathaniel, Lord, 99, 117, 102n1
  Partition of Bengal, 7, 67, 99–100, 131. *See also* Swadeshi movement

Deb, Radhakanta, 8
Devi, Hiranmoyee, 158n23
Devi, Jnanadanandini, 148, 149, 157n19, 166, 172n31. *See also* Balak

175

176 Index

Devi, Neepomoyee, 150, 158n24
Devi, Pratibha, 150, 159n25
Devi, Rassundari, 4, 8
Devi, Sarada 4, 158n21. *See also*
  Devi, Swarnakumari; Tagore,
  Debendranath
Devi, Swarnakumari, 141–45, 147–48,
  151. *See also* antahpur; dress;
  education
  on colonized, 3, 9–14, 24, 81–82,
    98–102
  on education, 5, 7, 9–10, 90,
    105–06
  on employment, 1–3, 12, 77–78,
    98–102
  on freedom, 6, 9–13, 15, 49–51,
    88–91, 148, 151
  the past, 6–7, 14–15
  on rights, 11–12, 74–75, 80,
    82–83
dress, xii, 9, 45, 49–50, 92–97,
  137–39, 146, 150. *See also*
  anthapur; Devi, Swarnakumari
Dutta, Hirendranath, 161, 169n6

education, x, 8, 22, 28, 70, 76, 90,
  104–06, 153. *See also* antahpur;
  Bethune School
  and English, 4–5, 20, 81, 82,
    145–46, 150
  as fulfilment, 5, 28, 76
  and Hindu custom, 27–28, 77.
    See also kulin/Kulinism
  and home, ix, 3, 5, 20–21, 47–49,
    71–75
  and Muslims, ix, 7, 131
  and opposition, 46, 48, 61, 70, 74,
    78, 84–85, 105
  and public domain, 6, 11–12, 14,
    49, 145
  and Tagore household, 138–46.
    See also Tagore, Debendranath;
    Tagore, Hemendranath; Tagore,
    Satyendranath

and texts, 6, 70, 140, 143
and westernization, 8–10, 20, 50,
  60
and women graduates, 97, 103,
  156n15, 161, 170n17

Fourth World Conference on Women,
  Beijing, 1995, 1

Ganguly, Manilal, 140, 154n2
gender, x–xi, xiii, 1–3, 9, 15. *See also*
  patriarchy
Ghare Baire, 15
girl child, 28–29, 115–16. *See also*
  child marriage; education

Indian National Congress, 131,
  140

Khastagir, Kumudini, 163, 168
kulins/Kulinism, 22, 23, 25n3, 28–29,
  34–37, 53n3, 56
  Ballal Sen, 25n3, 29, 53n1
  child marriage, 37–38, 40–42,
    46
  Kulinkulasarvasya, 145
  naikashya, shrotiya, 31–32
  tri-kulins, 33–35
  wives, 30–32, 35–37

love, 46–47, 52–53, 68, 79–80,
  105–06

The *Mahabharata*, 33, 53n5, 93, 110,
  130, 143n5
Maharashtra, as ideal, 40, 94, 158
marriage, 6, 52–53. *See also* child
  marriage; kulins/Kulinism
  and Brahmoism, 17, 147
  8 forms, xii, 56–57, 58n2
  writers' age at, 8.
  men, 105–07, 114. *See also* education;
    kulins/Kulinism

modernity, 8–14. *See also* Brahmo
    Samaj; Sen, Keshabchandra;
    Tagore, Satyendranath
Mozoomdar, Pratapchandra, 113–15,
    119n5

Nababidhan sect, 112, 119n5. *See also*
    Sen, Keshabchandra
Nari Shilpashala, 123–29

Parsees, 82, 148. *See also* dress
Partition of Bengal, 1905, 7, 98,
    103n2, 131, 171n31. *See also*
    Swadeshi movement
patriarchy, xiv, 2, 13, 16, 28. *See also*
    education; gender
purdah, 116–18

the *Ramayana*, 93, 144, 145
Ray, Sarala, 167, 173n35
Roy, Rammohan, 5, 6, 24n1, 146.
    See also Brahmoism; Brahmo
    Samaj

Sarkar, Mahendralal, 164, 171n25
Sen, Dineshchandra, 161–62, 169n11
Sen, Keshabchandra, 114, 119n5, 147,
    156n14, 157n16. *See also*
    Tagore, Debendranath;
    Nababidhan
Swadeshi movement, xiii, 7, 14–16,
    100–02, 129, 131–35

Tagore, Debendranath. *See also*
    Brahmoism
    and Brahmo Samaj, 29n1
    on education, 146–47. *See also*
        Devi, Swarnakumari
    on reform, 146–49
    and Sarala Devi Chaudhurani, 13,
        166–67, 172n30
Tagore, Dwarakanath, Prince, 142,
    154n5
Tagore, Gaganendranath, 167,
    173n33
Tagore Girindranath, 146, 156n13
Tagore Hemendranath, 147, 159,
    157n19
Tagore, Rabindranath, 122, 124,
    160–61, 163, 165
Tagore, Satyendranath, 147, 148–52,
    157n17, 158n20, 166, 170n12.
    See also Devi, Jnandanandini

University of Calcutta Act,
    1904, 99, 103n3

Vidyasagar, Iswarchandra, x, 144,
    154n7

widows, 23, 51–52, 53n4, 57, 62
women, 15, 136n1, 139
    as abala, 48, 49, 53n7
    as bama, 48
    as daughter-in-law, 39, 62, 153,
        166. *See also* kulin/Kulinism
    and Englishwomen, 14, 50
    and education, x–xii, 21, 107, 144,
        147. *See also* education
    and equality. *See* Tagore,
        Satyendranath
    and marriage. *See* child marriage;
        kulin/Kulinism
    as widows. *See* widows
    as wives, xi, 16, 21–22, 46, 68, 69,
        82–85. *See also* kulins/Kulinism

About the Editors and the Translators

Editors

MALINI BHATTACHARYA is an author, scholar, translator, playwright and activist in the women's movement. She retired as Professor of English and former Director, School of Women's Studies, Jadavpur University. She was a Member of Parliament, CPIM, 1989–1996.

ABHIJIT SEN retired as Publications Officer, School of Women's Studies, Jadavpur University.

Translators

BARNITA BAGCHI is Associate Professor in Comparative Literature at the Department of Languages, Literature and Communication, Utrecht University.

JASODHARA BAGCHI was the late Founder-Director of the School of Women's Studies, Jadavpur University and former Chairperson, West Bengal Commission for Women.

SOURIN BHATTACHARYA retired as Professor of Economics, Jadavpur University.

KUMARDEB BOSE retired as a research scientist and consultant in the field of chemistry.

SUPRIYA CHAUDHURI is Professor Emerita, Department of English, Jadavpur University.

SARBANI CHOUDHURY was Professor, Department of English, Kalyani University.

SUBHA CHAKRABORTY Dasgupta retired as Professor, Department of Comparative Literature, Jadavpur University.

AMLAN DASGUPTA retired as Professor, Department of English, Jadavpur University.

SARMISTHA DUTTA Gupta is a Kolkata-based feminist historian, writer and activist.

SWATI GANGULY is Professor, Department of English, Visva Bharati, Santiniketan.

CHANDRAYEE NIYOGI was Professor, Department of English, Jadavpur University.

MODHUMITA ROY is Associate Professor of English, Tufts University.